THE FIRST-YEAR
Seminar

**Designing, Implementing, and Assessing Courses
to Support Student Learning and Success**

**Assessing
First-Year
Seminars**

Volume Five

Daniel B. Friedman

NATIONAL RESOURCE CENTER
FIRST-YEAR EXPERIENCE® AND STUDENTS IN TRANSITION
UNIVERSITY OF SOUTH CAROLINA

Cite as:

Friedman, D. B. (2012). *The first-year seminar: Designing, implementing, and assessing courses to support student learning and success: Vol. V. Assessing first-year seminars.* Columbia, SC: University of South Carolina, National Resource Center for The First-Year Experience and Students in Transition.

Production Staff for the National Resource Center:
Series Editor   Tracy L. Skipper, Assistant Director for Publications
Design and Production   Josh Tyler, Graphic Artist

Library of Congress Cataloging-in-Publication Data
Keup, Jennifer R.
  The first-year seminar : designing, implementing, and assessing courses to support student learning & success / Jennifer R. Keup and Joni Webb Petschauer.
      p. cm.
  Includes bibliographical references.
  ISBN 978-1-889271-81-1
  1. College freshmen--United States. 2. College student orientation--United States. 3. Interdisciplinary approach in education--United States. I. Petschauer, Joni Webb. II. Title.
  LB2343.32.K48 2011
  378.1'98--dc22
                          2011015354

Contents

List of Tables and Figures

Notes on the Series

In this final volume of *The First-Year Seminar: Designing, Implementing, and Assessing Courses to Support Student Learning and Success,* Dan Friedman argues that we need to move beyond simply looking at retention and graduation rates and student satisfaction when assessing the first-year seminar. In reflecting on this volume, I thought it might be useful to briefly examine what we know about the assessment of these courses and suggest where examinations of the seminar might move in the future.

Since the early 1990s, the National Resource Center has collected and published approximately 140 campus-based reports on the outcomes associated with the first-year seminar (Barefoot, 1993; Barefoot, Warnock, Dickinson, Richardson, & Roberts, 1998; Griffin & Romm, 2008; Tobolowsky, Cox, & Wagner, 2005). Just over 60% of the research reports examined the seminar's impact on retention, and a little less than half focused on academic performance as measured by grade point average. Other frequently assessed course outcomes included student satisfaction with the seminar, its components, or with the institution (26.1%); self-assessment of learning or personal development (19.7%); or involvement or engagement with the academic and/or social life of the campus (19.0%). Less frequently assessed outcomes included academic progress as measured by credits attempted and/or credits earned, graduation rates, academic and career decision making, academic skills, course structure and instructional strategies, use of campus services, attitudes toward or understanding of higher education or important social values, impact on course instructors, and financial impact of the course. In a relatively few cases, institutions examined the differential impact of the seminar on retention and/or academic performance by race or ethnicity, gender, or academic preparation.

The assessment practices described in these research reports mirror those reported by respondents to the 2009 National Survey of First-Year Seminars (Padgett & Keup, 2011). Here the four most commonly reported assessment outcomes were (a) persistence to sophomore year (73.7%), (b) satisfaction with faculty (70.9%), (c) satisfaction with the institution (65.3%), and (d) grade point average (58.0%). Interestingly, only 15.5% of respondents to that survey identified improving sophomore return rates (i.e., retention) as an important course objective. However, other objectives, such as developing a connection with the institution (50.2%), providing an orientation to campus resources and services (47.6%), developing a support network (17.4%), and increasing student-faculty interactions (16.9%), could be interpreted as fitting under the retention umbrella.

The overriding emphasis on retention, academic performance, and satisfaction is not difficult to understand. After all, these are relatively easy data to collect, analyze, and report. First-year seminars are instituted on many campuses to respond to concerns about retention; thus, examining the impact of the seminar on persistence to the second semester, the second year, and beyond is not surprising. Yet, once the seminar has been established as having a positive impact on retention (or academic performance or satisfaction), what else is there to learn? Plenty—as suggested by Friedman's work here. For example, we might examine which aspects of the seminar (e.g., instructional strategies, course content, use of peer leaders, grading policies, class size) have the greatest impact on these outcomes, or we might look at the differential impact of the seminar vis-à-vis these outcomes on various groups of students. As accrediting bodies and local, state, and federal governments have begun to pay increasing attention to not only whether institutions are graduating students but also to what those students know and can do upon graduation, it becomes increasingly important to examine the impact of the seminar on a wide range of learning and personal development outcomes.

Demonstrating that seminars are successful is essential to their continued presence on college and university campuses, but knowing why they are successful and how they might be made more so is vital to the academic and personal success of the current and future students enrolled in them. Thus, it is not really surprising that each volume in this series has touched on some aspect of assessing the first-year seminar. In volume I, Keup and Petschauer described the role of assessment in developing and launching a seminar, but they also noted its importance in managing change within the course and ensuring its institutionalization. Groccia and Hunter in volume II explored the assessment and evaluation of instruction as a professional development activity, yet it can also help explain how and why certain course outcomes are being achieved. Similarly, evaluation of instruction can suggest why progress on key objectives is flagging and identify a focus for future faculty development and training events.

In volume III, Garner offered suggestions for nontraditional assessments of student learning. While assessments based on student performance (e.g., presentations, portfolios, essays) rather than recall (e.g., tests and quizzes) may give us better insight into what students know and can do, they can also form an important component of programmatic assessment. In volume IV, Latino and Ashcraft provided a 360-degree plan for assessing the peer leader component of the first-year seminar, evaluating the impact of the peer leadership on the students served, on the peers themselves, and on the overall effectiveness of the course. The current volume brings those disparate pieces together in a comprehensive assessment plan for the seminar.

As such, I close the series with a sense that we have come full circle. Assessing a pilot course is essential to the launch of a first-year seminar program. Once the course is established, ongoing assessment efforts point to the need to revisit major aspects of the seminar. For example, what new topics should be addressed or activities incorporated into instructor training? Which teaching strategies need to be more widely adopted to help students meet key learning outcomes and improve satisfaction with the course? Which strategies could be deemphasized? How can peer leaders be used more effectively to support their own learning and development and that of the students they serve? My hope is that as readers conduct assessment of the first-year seminar on their campuses, they will be drawn back to the earlier volumes in the series for ideas on how to make use of what they are learning.

I began this piece with the suggestion that we need to broaden our assessment horizon with respect to the first-year seminar. Yet, I also want to note that we need to increase assessment activity—period. When respondents to the 2009 National Survey of First-Year Seminar were asked whether the course had been formally assessed in the previous three years, about one third reported that it had not been, and another 10% indicated they did not know whether it had been assessed (Padgett & Keup, 2011). Clearly, the majority of these courses are being assessed, but the possibility that 30–40% of colleges and universities may not be assessing the first-year seminar is a concern.

The need for more and broader assessment studies suggests two key purposes for this book. The first is to help those who are launching a new seminar or who have never formally assessed the seminar to come up with a plan for doing so. For those readers with assessed seminars, the book can offer strategies for refining current assessment plans. Hopefully, it will inspire these readers to consider new questions about the seminar, moving beyond asking whether the seminar is working to asking why and how it is working.

As Friedman notes, the prospect of conducting assessment can prove daunting. It is my hope that his work will demystify that process for readers. As always, we welcome your feedback on this book and on the other volumes in the series.

Tracy L. Skipper
Series Editor
National Resource Center for The First-Year Experience and
Students in Transition
University of South Carolina

Introduction

For much of its history, higher education has taken what Hersch (2005) described as a faith-based approach to assessment. That is, it has taken on faith that what we do works. This is obviously no longer acceptable, as colleges and universities are under increasing pressure from external and internal forces, most notably the federal government, regional accrediting bodies, parents, students, and the general public, to demonstrate their effectiveness.

Assessment is imperative for other reasons. In addition to demonstrating to others what we are doing, assessment (a) assists in funding requests; (b) informs planning and decision making; (c) helps us make inferences about the overall quality of a program or educational approach; (d) allows us to celebrate our success; and (e) most importantly, provides a method of continuous improvement whereby we can modify and improve our programs.

First-year seminars have a long history in the assessment movement and are often noted as being the most frequently assessed course or innovation in higher education (Tobolowsky, Cox, & Wagner, 2005; Upcraft, 2005). This perception may be due, in part, to the seminar's early history. When the University 101 course at the University of South Carolina—arguably, the genesis of the modern first-year seminar—was created, assessment was built into the fabric of the course. As early as 1972, studies were commissioned to assess the effectiveness of the experimental program (Heckel, Hiers, Finegold, & Zuidema, 1973). Throughout the 1970s and 1980s, course administrators conducted numerous assessments on University 101 to provide evidence of its effectiveness to the Faculty Senate, which approved the course. Results of these assessments found that the course was associated with higher retention and graduation rates, as well as better grades (Heckel et al., 1973; Morris & Cutright, 2005). The desire to use research methods to evaluate the merits of an educational program is an early example of the assessment movement, though it is interesting to note that the same level of scrutiny was not applied to other courses at the University. First-year seminars were, and continue to be, held to higher standards than other academic courses (Swing, 2001).

The positive assessment findings of University 101 led to the establishment of the first-year seminar as an accepted and valued curricular component at the University of South Carolina. An additional outcome was the rapid growth of first-year seminars across the nation; according to the 2009 National Survey of First-Year Seminars, 87% of responding institutions noted they offered such a course on their campuses (Padgett & Keup, 2011).

While seminars are becoming more ubiquitous, assessment of these courses has not kept pace with their growth. In a 2001 monograph on assessing the first college year, Swing noted assessment of first-year programs was frequently limited to either surveys of student satisfaction or correlation analyses of participation and retention. While these are important metrics, they do not tell the full story of how successful a seminar is or what can be done to make necessary improvements. In the decade that followed Swing's criticism, not much progress was made in improving the sophistication of first-year seminar assessment plans. According to the 2009 National Survey of First-Year Seminars, just over half (56.5%) of the institutions indicating they offered a first-year seminar also reported that it had been formally assessed since 2006 (Padgett & Keup, 2011). As these authors noted, of the seminars that were assessed, most focused on simple and "easily acquired outcomes, such as retention rates and satisfaction measures, regardless of their alignment with stated goals of the seminar" (p. 56).

The focus on persistence as the primary assessment metric is understandable given the continued importance of retaining students on an institution's bottom line and the increased attention to this by external audiences. However, while retention is important, it is only one piece of a much larger strategy. Given the higher standards to which these seminars are generally held, as well as the climate of accountability surrounding higher education, having a thoughtful and thorough assessment plan for such courses is critical. If first-year seminars are to continue to thrive, improvements must be made in how they are assessed. The focus must widen from retention, graduation rates, and satisfaction to include direct measures of learning, evidence of the extent to which course learning outcomes were achieved, and a variety of lenses and perspectives to interpret the data. In addition, assessment should widen to include other stakeholders, such as faculty, campus partners, and former students. Most importantly, seminar leaders need to do a better job of putting data into action in order to make programmatic improvements. In essence, seminar leaders need to focus not just on proving that the seminar matters, but also on improving the experience each year (Swing, 2001).

Assessment is often challenging for first-year seminar administrators. Many questions continue to confound the leaders of these courses. Who and what should be assessed? How? When? Once we have findings, how should they be interpreted? This book seeks to provide practical advice and guidance in answering these questions.

Chapter 1 provides an overview of assessment, including various definitions and uses. In addition, a new model for assessing a first-year seminar is proposed. Several lenses for interpreting data are explained, including criterion-based, benchmarking, longitudinal, and value-added. A few major assessment designs, such as experimental and quasi-experimental, are provided to frame an understanding for how assessments might be structured. The chapter closes with important notes about the limitations of assessment.

Building on the discussion of value-added assessment in the opening chapter, chapter 2 uses Astin's (1993) Inputs-Environment-Outcomes model as a way of thinking about who and what to assess. The chapter begins with an explanation of this value-added assessment model and discusses ways in which programs and institutions have typically misapplied it, focusing on portions of the model rather than using it as an integrated whole. The chapter then breaks the model down into its three components (i.e., inputs, environment, and outcomes) and relates how they apply to assessing a first-year seminar. The discussion of inputs highlights ways to understand the pre-enrollment characteristics of students and how these might impact the assessment of outcomes. A brief overview of the environmental factors that could contribute to the intended outcomes follows. A list of the most typically assessed outcomes of first-year seminars and an organizing taxonomy provides guidance on what to assess. The chapter concludes with a thorough discussion of how to write clear and measurable learning outcomes. Examples from various institutions are provided.

Chapters 3 and 4 highlight techniques, methods, and strategies for assessing a first-year seminar, with a particular emphasis on data collection. The first of these chapters focuses on the *how* of assessment. It distinguishes between and offers guidance on using direct and indirect measures of student learning. Both quantitative and qualitative methods are discussed. The chapter also provides advice when considering whether programs should design their own surveys or use national instruments. Best practices in developing survey items are provided. In addition, sample rubrics for assessing student learning are offered. Chapter 4 focuses on the *who* of assessment, that is, the individuals whose experiences form the basis of programmatic assessment. It provides an overview of sampling techniques and a discussion of strategies for increasing response rates. The chapter closes with ideas for other populations relevant to first-year seminars that could be assessed.

Chapter 5 offers advice and recommendations for analyzing, interpreting, and using assessment results. Reporting findings and applying them to practice are perhaps the most critical and overlooked aspects of the assessment process. There is often a rush to collect and analyze data, without much forethought as to how it will be used, with whom it will be shared, or what will be done with the information learned. Data have to be put into action for assessment to be useful. This chapter discusses how to effectively disaggregate, interpret, use, and report assessment findings.

The volume concludes with a discussion of the course review process as a natural starting point for assessment and as a strategy for refining learning outcomes and assessment plans. Chapter 6 also offers some brief closing reflections on the best practices for first-year seminar assessment.

Chapter 1
An Overview of First-Year Seminar Assessment

For many higher education professionals, assessment can be an intimidating endeavor. Yet, from a macro perspective, assessment is really quite simple, if one has the right prescription (Rx). When it comes down to it, what we are really doing is determining the level of Relevance and Excellence of our programs. Relevance means, *Are we doing the right things?* In turn, excellence suggests, *Are we doing things right?* Assessment helps us determine the answer to these important questions.

This chapter draws on several definitions of assessment to clarify its scope and purpose. A comprehensive model for assessing first-year seminars is proposed. In addition, a distinction is made between assessment as a process for summative and formative purposes. The chapter closes with an explanation of several lenses through which data can be interpreted and a note about the limitations and realities of campus-based assessment work.

What Is Assessment?

As a relatively new field, the terms and definitions of assessment are still in flux. Every book on assessment offers a new, and slightly contradictory, definition of assessment. Palomba and Banta (1999), drawing on the work of Marchese, defined assessment as "the systematic collection, review, and use of information about educational programs undertaken for the purpose of improving student learning and development" (p. 4). Similarly, Angelo (1995) described assessment as "an ongoing process aimed at understanding and improving student learning" (p. 7). While clear and succinct, these definitions may be too narrow. To focus exclusively on student learning is to ignore the many other benefits and outcomes related to the educational enterprise. For a first-year seminar, these other outcomes might include the impact of teaching on the instructor, the personal and professional development of serving as a peer educator, or the impact of the course on campus partners.

While these definitions focus on student learning, it is important to note that for the purposes of this book, it is the educational program being assessed rather than individual students. Thus, while information is collected on and from students, it will be used in the aggregate to make judgments about or improvements to the program. In other words, the unit of analysis is the individual student or course section, but the focus is on the larger seminar program.

A broader definition of assessment was offered by Upcraft and Schuh (1996), who defined it as "any effort to gather, analyze, and interpret evidence" (p. 18) related to program effectiveness. The authors distinguished between assessment and evaluation, commenting that program evaluation is "any effort to use assessment evidence to improve institutional, departmental, divisional, or agency effectiveness" (p. 19). Further, they characterized assessment as describing program effectiveness, while evaluation was seen as the process of using those descriptions to make judgments or changes.

Maki (2004) offered yet another definition, stating "assessing for learning is a systematic and systemic process of inquiry into what and how well students learn over the progression of their studies and is driven by intellectual curiosity about the efficacy of collective educational practices" (p. xvii). Her model (Figure 1.1) suggests assessment is a natural phenomenon employed daily

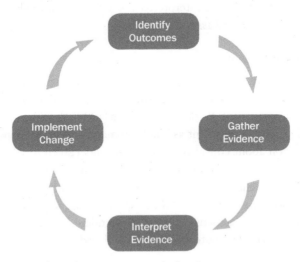

Figure 1.1. Maki's (2004) assessment cycle (p. 5).

in our lives. Tasks as basic as driving to work require a simplified version of the assessment process. For example, if the intended outcome is to get to work on time without a speeding ticket, the driver will gather evidence using the speedometer as the source of data. Next the driver interprets the data. If the speedometer reads 90 miles per hour, the interpretation is, "that is too fast, better slow down." Now, the driver needs to make changes based on the interpretation, which would involve taking his or her foot off the accelerator. The technicalities in assessing first-year seminars will obviously be more involved and complicated, but the general principle is the same. Assessment is simply articulating the outcomes to be accomplished, gathering evidence related to the outcomes, determining the extent to which they were accomplished, and then making changes based on the interpretation of the evidence.

One shortcoming of Maki's model is that, in conveying the continual nature of the assessment cycle, the arrow moving from implementing change to identifying outcomes may be a bit misleading. Often, it is not necessary to revisit the outcomes; rather, program administrators need to rethink the methods of achieving the outcomes. It may not be the outcome that needs "fixing" but the process of accomplishing the outcome. For example, do faculty receive adequate training and support to accomplish their work in the seminar? If not, the seminar may be less likely to achieve outcomes related to student learning and development. In this case, program administrators would need to make changes to the faculty development agenda rather than the seminar outcomes.

A revision of Maki's cycle offers a more accurate and relevant model for assessing a first-year seminar (Figure 1.2). The process begins with defining the intended outcomes of the program or service. To borrow an expression from Covey (1989), we begin with the end in mind. This includes defining student learning outcomes, but it may also involve identifying the potential impact of the course on other constituents, such as instructors, peer leaders, or campus partners. Once program administrators know what they are trying to accomplish, they can design the program, service, or intervention—in this case, the first-year seminar. Because the course is only as good as the instructor, faculty preparation to achieve course learning outcomes becomes a logical next step. During and following the seminar, data relevant to the program and outcomes can be collected. These include direct or indirect measures, using qualitative or quantitative methods, and so on. Analysis and interpretation follow data collection. Here, program directors decide what the data mean and what they should do with what they learned. In step 6 of the model, data are used to make a judgment about and/or to improve the program, which could entail clarifying or refining intended outcomes, making informed adjustments to the course, and/or making changes to the faculty development efforts to better ensure seminar instructors are focusing on what works and what matters.

At this point in the process, the information about the findings and planned changes should be shared with others. Sharing information with valued stakeholders is helpful for processing the implications and determining what to do with the findings. It may also assist program administrators refine proposed changes and build buy-in for moving the course in new directions. A final component of the model involves mandatory reporting to either internal or external constituents. Here, a dotted line suggests that offering summative data for compliance purposes does not necessarily lead to formative improvements and is, thus, technically outside the assessment cycle.

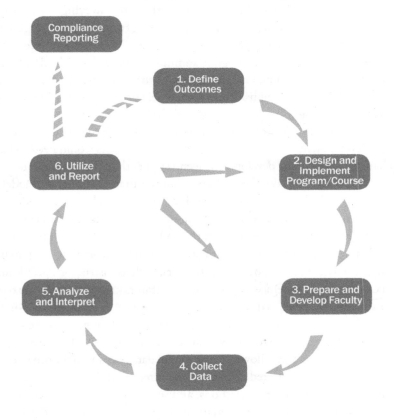

Figure 1.2. First-year seminar assessment cycle: A revision of Maki (2004).

Distinction Between Assessment and Research

While good assessment will draw on many of the principles and methods of social science research, the two processes differ in both purpose and scope. The purpose of research is to test theory and concepts, while assessment is designed to inform practice. In addition, assessment generally focuses on a single institution, while research is intended to be generalized to larger contexts (Erwin, 1991; Upcraft & Schuh, 1996). Further, Upcraft (2005) noted that assessment studies often cannot match the necessary rigor required of social science research due to time and resource limitations.

Uses of Assessment

It is important to draw a distinction between the two primary uses or purposes for assessment. On the one hand, assessment can be used to make a judgment or evaluation about the efficacy of a program. As such, *summative* assessment is typically conducted at the end of the experience. Alternately, assessment can provide feedback to continually form or improve the program or course. *Formative* assessments can be conducted during (e.g., midsemester evaluation) or after (e.g., end-of-course evaluation, survey of former students) the experience.

Underlying these primary uses are two paradigms of assessment: (a) the improvement paradigm and (b) the accountability paradigm (Ewell, 2009). These frameworks are helpful for understanding how the differing purposes of assessment will impact data collection, analysis, and reporting. The *improvement paradigm* is, as the name suggests, focused internally on formative program enhancements. The primary ethos of the improvement paradigm is one of engagement, rather than compliance. In the improvement paradigm, evidence can be collected from various sources ranging from exams, projects, portfolios, or other course-embedded assessments and using various methods (i.e., quantitative or qualitative). The *accountability paradigm* is externally focused and concerned with making summative judgments about a program. It relies primarily, if not exclusively, on quantitative methods, particularly standardized tests. Steps 4 through 6 of the assessment model described in Figure 1.2 are dictated by the paradigm employed. In other words, the ways in which data are collected, interpreted, and used will depend on the ultimate purpose of the assessment.

Interpreting Findings—Using Multiple Lenses

It can be quite complicated to answer a seemingly easy question such as, How are we doing? A hypothetical assessment finding helps illustrate the complexity in extracting meaning from results. Improved critical-thinking skills are a desired outcome for many first-year seminars. An institution might use any number of instruments to measure this outcome. Yet, knowing that seminar students at the college or university score 5.2 on a 7.0 scale for critical thinking may not indicate whether the seminar is successful. To determine that, it would be helpful to know what score is considered good, what the scores were last year, how similar institutions fared, and whether the students are improving. Having several reference points or lenses for the data will help make sense of the extent to which the program is successful.

Suskie (2004) identified four lenses that can be used to frame and interpret data, which are described below.

» *Standards-based lenses,* also known as criterion-referenced, tell how student(s) performed against a predetermined standard. In the example above, the mean (average) score for critical thinking was 5.2. In the absence of a standard, it is hard to know whether it is good or bad. Learning that a score of 5.5 is considered good provides some meaning.

Standards can be set internally, by an outside agency, or by the designer of the assessment instrument. For example, the First-Year Initiative Assessment, sponsored by Educational Benchmarking Incorporated, defines good performance as a mean of 5.5 on a 7-point scale.

Before setting an internal standard for a particular measure, it might be prudent to collect baseline data. Having a better understanding of the current level of performance is critical for setting meaningful targets for future performance. Otherwise, initial attempts are nothing more than a shot in the dark.

» *Peer-referenced data,* also known as benchmarking, suggest how a program compares against a peer group. It provides a sense of relative standing. In the hypothetical scenario, it is of limited use to simply know that the mean of 5.2 is not quite at the level of good. It would be more helpful to know how the seminar compares to similar programs at other institutions. Knowing that the average score for the peer group was 4.9 may change the context for interpreting a score of 5.2.

Selecting a peer group for an intervention like the first-year seminar can be challenging. Institutions often have a thoughtfully crafted peer group for comparing faculty salaries, tuition levels, and academic achievement. Many offices of institutional research have a list of peer institutions that can be used to compare the seminar against; however, while the institutions may be similar, the seminar characteristics may not be. For first-year seminars, it is helpful to compare apples to apples—that is, seminars of similar purpose, scope, and structure. Any of the following factors might provide a basis for identifying a peer group: type of seminar (e.g., extended orientation, academic, basic study skills, preprofessional), number of credit hours, how the seminar is graded (A-F, pass/fail, no grade), type of institution, and number of students in the first-year cohort.

» *Longitudinal data*[1] suggest whether scores are getting better. For example, maybe the score of 5.2 was up from 4.3 the year before. This finding certainly would suggest the program is moving in the right direction. But can this gain be attributed to improvements in the program? Perhaps the increased scores are due to admitting a brighter or more motivated cohort of students. To more fully attribute gains to a specific intervention, a value-added lens should be used.

» *The value-added lens* suggests whether the students are improving as a result of specific interventions. Rather than measuring different cohorts to assess change, value-added assessment measures growth within one group of students. In the hypothetical scenario, value-added assessment may indicate the critical-thinking score for entering students was 4.0, and the score at the end of the first semester, for the same group of students, increased to 5.2.

Assessment Designs

Used singly, the lenses described above provide only a limited perspective on how a program is doing. To better understand program efficacy, it is important to use multiple lenses. Similarly, the results of any assessment process are only as good as the design used to gather data. Four of the designs used most frequently to frame an assessment study are described below: (a) experimental, (b) quasi-experimental, (c) modified experimental, and (d) single-group designs.

---

[1] This book draws on the work of Suskie (2004) in defining longitudinal research, where the performance of one cohort may be compared to that of an earlier cohort. Other scholars often define longitudinal research as following the same cohort of students over a period a time.

Experimental

Considered the gold standard of assessment design (Pike, 2009), experimental designs involve the random assignment of students to a treatment or nontreatment group (Figure 1.3). With random assignment, the differences in outcomes can be directly attributed to level of participation in the intervention, because all other student characteristics and experiences vary randomly. Unfortunately, due to ethical and practical considerations, these designs are rarely feasible or appropriate in educational settings.

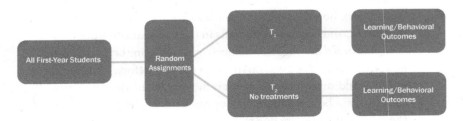

Figure 1.3. Experimental design.

Quasi-Experimental

This type of design uses naturally formed groups to compare participants against nonparticipants. At institutions that do not require a first-year seminar, this design would compare students who enrolled in the course to those who did not. While this analysis can account for many of the variables—in addition to participation in the seminar—that explain change over time, it is not fully possible to eliminate *volunteer bias* (i.e., individuals who choose to participate in an experience may differ in some fundamental and particularly significant ways from those who do not choose to participate) from the equation. A more detailed explanation of statistical controls that can be used to account for the absence of random assignment can be found in Pike's (2009) work.

Modified Experimental

A compromise possibility can occur when an elective seminar has more student demand than it can accommodate (Figure 1.4). Students who desire to participate but are turned away can comprise a valuable control group. Thus, three groups are effectively created: T_1—enrolled students, T_2—students who wanted to enroll but were denied enrollment, and T_3—students who did not wish to enroll. T_2 is a perfect control group for T_1 because it mediates effects of volunteer bias.

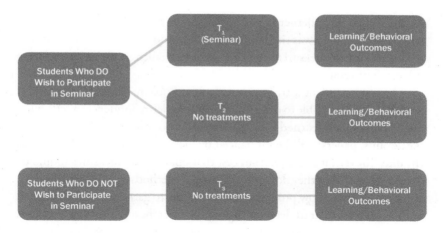

Figure 1.4. Modified experimental design.

Designs Without Control Groups

According to the 2009 National Survey of First-Year Seminars, 54% of responding institutions offered a seminar that was required of all students (Padgett & Keup, 2011). This makes assessment a bit more challenging as there is no comparison group. Elective courses can evaluate gains by comparing participants with nonparticipants, but this comparison is not possible if the course is required. In this case, options would be to compare the program with peer institutions (benchmarking) or track results over time (longitudinal).

The Limits of Assessment

Walvoord (2004) noted, "educational situations contain too many variables to make 'proof' possible. Therefore, assessment gathers indicators that will be useful for decision making" (p. 2). Most analyses of assessment data use inferential statistics, which, as the name implies, only allow us to make inferences about the data, not to suggest absolute conclusions. Further, what is often believed are precise quantitative findings actually contain a great deal of uncertainty, mainly due to random error. Mlodinow (2008) suggests there will always be a degree of error that is simply related to the timing of data collection. If the same measurement was repeated two days in a row, slightly different results might be found. Student responses to course evaluations or instruments regarding satisfaction, engagement, or experiences at the institution could be influenced by extraneous factors, such as whether an assignment was returned that day, whether the cafeteria worker smiled in the food court, or whether the student was tired or hungry. Mlodinow went on to suggest that the uncertainty in measurement becomes more challenging when considering subjective criteria.

Assessing student learning is even more problematic. As Suskie (2004) noted, "it is not possible to determine with complete confidence exactly what our students have learned" (p. 19). Performance on measures of learning (i.e., exams, papers) will be influenced by luck, illness, memory lapses, and the like. These cautions do not suggest that quantitative measures should be done away with, but they do imply that mixed-methods approaches are advisable because they allow program administrators to gather enough data of all kinds to deepen their understanding of program efficacy. The more methods used, the greater the chances of garnering a more accurate snapshot of reality.

Conclusion

Regardless of the methods employed, there is no ideal assessment design. As with a social science or educational research study, there is no way to design a perfect assessment plan that isolates a program and controls for all extraneous factors. While it is easy to feel overwhelmed by all the considerations necessary for effective assessment, it is still important and necessary to make incremental progress in understanding the extent to which our programs are successful, for whom, how, and why. As Astin et al. (1996) noted in the American Association of Higher Education's nine principles of good practice for assessing student learning, the power of assessment is in the cumulative nature of the ongoing process. Every time an assessment cycle is completed, strategies are refined and perspectives gained on emerging questions, and our understanding about what works and why it works is improved. Thus, one-shot assessments will not yield the depth of understanding necessary to accurately and fully understand our programs.

Chapter 2
A Framework for Assessing a First-Year Seminar

Chapter 1 described several different lenses that can be used as a guide for designing assessment plans. This chapter examines one of those lenses—value-added assessment—in greater depth. Astin's (1993) Input-Environment-Outcome (IEO) model is a classic example of value-added assessment for educational interventions. The IEO model will serve as a framework for understanding the basic components of an effective assessment design. Before examining the model in the context of first-year seminar assessment, the chapter will address some of the shortcomings of common assessment efforts. Considerable attention will also be given to crafting student learning outcomes.

Value-Added Assessment Design

Astin's (1993) IEO model (Figure 2.1) is an assessment framework that allows one to identify the extent to which a given environment (i.e., treatment or experience) contributes to an outcome, while accounting for relevant input variables that may also influence or explain the outcome. It is a useful model for assessing change over time and examining the possible causes of change.

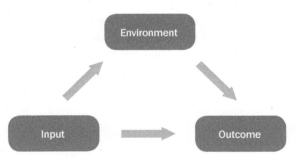

Figure 2.1. Astin's (1993) Input-Environment-Outcome Assessment Model.

Student outcomes are associated with both the experiences they have while in college (environment) and the characteristics and talents they had prior to participating in a program (input). Before looking more specifically at each of these components, it might be helpful to consider the ways the model is sometimes applied incompletely to assess our students, programs, and institutions.

» *Measuring inputs.* Traditionally, measures of college prestige have been based largely on input measures, such as SAT scores, high school grades, or class rank. This is an example of incomplete assessment, where reputation or prestige is based on measures that occur before a student arrives at the college or university, rather than looking at what students actually learn while enrolled.

» *Measuring environment.* When focusing on the experience or program, simple counts or descriptions of activities are common. For instance, measuring the environment might involve reporting the number of participants enrolled in the first-year seminar, the amount of resources devoted to the seminar, or the number of students who completed an online alcohol unit. While these are important factors to consider, they do not in and of themselves suggest that they made any difference. Simply reporting that students participated in a given program does not necessarily mean it had any benefit.

» *Measuring outcomes.* Here, the focus may be on end results without regard to the causes of the results. Examples include retention rates, grades, or graduation rates. Again, these are important metrics. However, without linking them to the environment and input variables, the numbers do not mean much. Positive outcomes could be explained by positive inputs, rather than by any environmental variable.

» *Measuring environment to outcomes.* A program yielding a 97% one-year retention rate, a 3.5 grade point average, and a 90% four-year graduation rate for enrolled students would undoubtedly be touted as a success. Many campuses have such a program—it is called an Honors College. Students in these programs may have average SAT scores over 1400 and high school GPAs above 4.0. Thus, a large part of the successful outcomes may be due to the input variables rather than the environment. Without knowing relevant characteristics of students as they enter the environment, it is hard to determine whether the educational experience really contributed much to the outcome.

» *Measuring input to outcome.* Looking at the change from input to outcomes without accounting for environment merely suggests change or growth, but not impact. It is possible to know that change occurred, but not why or how.

As these examples of incomplete assessment make clear, looking at only part of the equation does not suggest that a given environment has contributed to student learning. To understand the impact of a program, outcomes must be measured in terms of who students are when they enroll (i.e., what they know, what they can do) and what environmental variables contributed to their experience. For instance, in order to assess the impact of a first-year seminar on a student's writing ability, input data (pretest) could be collected through a writing sample at summer orientation or through the SAT writing score. Students then participate in the seminar (environment) where they learn about and practice academic writing. Samples of students' work could be collected at the end of the semester and compared with the pretest writing sample to measure change over time.

IEO as a Framework for Assessing a First-Year Seminar

Employing the IEO model in its entirety provides a more complete understanding of the impact (outcome) of the first-year seminar (environment) on students. Here, some of the most common input variables examined by colleges and universities are considered. Characteristics of the seminar (e.g., course content, instruction, grading) become important environmental variables. Finally, some of the more commonly assessed outcomes associated with first-year seminars are described.

Inputs

Understanding who the students are before they enroll is important for two reasons: (a) it can help faculty and curriculum planners design the proper educational strategies, and (b) the relevant characteristics of entering students can be used as either baseline data or a statistical control to account for any pre-existing differences between groups (if comparing participants to nonparticipants or comparing one entering cohort to another). For assessment purposes, an input would be any pre-enrollment variable that could conceivably affect the outcome. Astin (1993) identified numerous possible input variables that could impact student achievement, including

» Academic preparedness, such as high school performance or SAT scores
» Demographics, such as gender, age, race, family income, or parental education
» Attitudes and behaviors
» Level of motivation
» Expectations regarding level of engagement in college
» Study skills and academic behaviors

To assess the impact of the first-year seminar, it is necessary to identify as many pre-enrollment factors as possible that could contribute to the outcomes being measured. For example, if measuring the effect the seminar has on writing skills, it is important to account for other variables that might explain how well a student writes. These could include verbal SAT score, English placement score, grade in senior English, or the essay score of the SAT or ACT. Another option is to administer a pretest, perhaps as the initial assignment in the seminar, to gather baseline data. In many cases, institutions probably have existing data sources that can be mined to gather important input variables, such as

» Admissions data, which might include predicted GPA, a metric frequently created by selective institutions as a way of establishing a cut point for admissions decisions. This figure is generally a function of a student's high school grades, class rank, and SAT or ACT score.
» Student data file information from the registrar's office, which includes grades, credit hours attempted or earned, and persistence and graduation variables.
» Aggregate data on incoming cohorts as well as survey data collected by institutional research offices. Some of the survey data collected by these offices may consist of the following:
  • *Freshman Survey (CIRP).* Administered to entering students prior to the start of the fall semester, this instrument measures pre-enrollment variables, including demographic characteristics; secondary school experiences; attitudes towards college; expectations of the college experience; degree goals and career plans; and attitudes, values, and life goals. This survey can be paired with other instruments from the Higher Education Research Institute (HERI), such as the Your First College Year (YFCY) or College Student Survey (CSS) to measure change over time.

- *College Student Inventory (CSI).* This nationally normed instrument, administered by Noel-Levitz, is designed to identify students' needs, attitudes, motivational patterns, resources, coping mechanisms, and receptivity to intervention.

- *College Student Expectations Questionnaire (CSXQ).* Adapted from the College Student Experiences Questionnaire (CSEQ), this pre-enrollment instrument is designed to evaluate new students' expectations for college, including their goals, motivations, and future plans for college experiences. Value-added assessments are possible by comparing results from the CSXQ with data from the CSEQ completed by the same students near the end of the first year or later in the college experience.

- *Beginning Survey of Student Engagement (BSSE).* Administered to entering students prior to the start of the fall semester, this instrument provides pre-enrollment data regarding engagement activities during the last year of high school and expectations about the level of engagement in the coming school year. When used with the National Survey of Student Engagement (NSSE), institutions can gain useful value-added data.

Environment

In research parlance, the environment is known as the intervention or treatment. Here, it is the educational program and the first-year seminar, specifically. Paying attention to the environment and experiences that are being assessed is critical because the best way to improve outcomes is to understand the experiences students have (Astin et al., 1996). While it is important to know whether the program is effective, it is even more important to know why. This is a missing piece in the literature on the success of first-year seminars. A great deal of collective evidence attests to the positive impact these courses have on grades and retention and graduation rates, but researchers have not been able to precisely identify which factors really contribute to these gains (Porter & Swing, 2006).

Unpacking the environmental influences allows program administrators to move beyond making general claims about the impact of a first-year seminar (or other intervention or environment) to highlighting specific subvariables that contribute to the observed outcomes. For example, the first-year seminar is frequently linked to increased retention, but what is known about the elements of the course that foster persistence? Any number or combination of variables might contribute to the retention effect, such as

- » Small class size
- » Out-of-class engagement
- » Faculty-student interaction
- » Positive peer interactions
- » Use of campus services
- » Exposure to a peer leader
- » Specific course content
- » Academic skill development

Is it enough to have a small class with a caring faculty member, or does the seminar need to address specific topics, such as time management, wellness, or responsible behaviors? Without this information, decisions might be made about what the seminar should do and how it should be done based on what is believed to be right, rather than on any empirical evidence. As Banta, Jones, and Black (2009) suggest, simply "measuring a desired outcome will do little to improve it without a look at the processes that led to the outcome" (p. 16). More information about disaggregating the environment is provided in chapter 5.

Outcomes

At the center of any assessment effort is the question, What are we measuring? According the 2009 National Survey of First-Year Seminars (Padgett & Keup, 2011), most first-year seminars focus on assessing persistence to sophomore year, satisfaction with faculty and the institution, and academic performance (Table 2.1). While these are important items to assess, they suggest little about actual learning or development.

Astin's (1993) taxonomy of outcomes is a useful alternative to thinking through the full range of possible outcomes to assess. According to the taxonomy, outcomes can be either (a) cognitive, that is, related to knowledge, skills, and mental processes, or (b) affective, which includes students' feelings, attitudes, beliefs, and relationships. In addition, data related to these outcomes can be broken into two categories: (a) psychological, which Astin defined as internal states or traits, and (b) behavioral. Figure 2.2 suggests possible outcomes for a first-year seminar organized using Astin's taxonomy.

Table 2.1

First-Year Seminar Assessment Outcomes (n = 357)

Outcome	Percent
Persistence to sophomore year	73.7
Satisfaction with faculty	70.9
Satisfaction with the institution	65.3
Grade point average	58.0
Use of campus services	51.0
Connections with peers	49.3
Participation in campus activities	49.0
Out-of-class student-faculty interaction	47.1
Academic abilities	42.0
Persistence to graduation	38.4
Other	18.5

Note. Reprinted from *2009 National Survey of First-Year Seminars: Ongoing Efforts to Support Students in Transition* (Research Reports on College Transitions No. 2) by R. D. Padgett and J. R. Keup, 2011, p. 55. Copyright 2011 by the University of South Carolina.

	Type of Data	Type of Outcome
	Cognitive	*Affective*

Psychological	Writing
	Speaking
	Reading
	Subject-matter
	  knowledge
	Critical thinking
		Values
		Satisfaction with
		  institution

Behavioral	GPA One-year persistence Degree attainment	Leadership Citizenship Time management Wellness Level of engagement Compliance with institutional policies

Figure 2.2. First-year seminar outcomes organized by Astin's (1993) taxonomy.

Cognitive-Behavioral outcomes generally encompass traditional academic aims, including the holy trinity of first-year outcomes: (a) academic performance (generally measured by grade point average), (b) retention and persistence rates (usually reported as first-to-second-year retention rates), and (c) graduation rates. While these are sometimes explicitly stated outcomes of a seminar, in many cases they are considered positive by-products of other types of outcomes.

Affective-Psychological outcomes may include satisfaction (either with the course or with the overall experience at the college or university), values clarification, and ethical reasoning.

Affective-Behavioral outcomes include measures such as level of engagement in the learning experience, the ability to manage time and priorities, appropriate behaviors regarding personal wellness (e.g., drug and alcohol use, amount of exercise), and compliance with university policies (e.g., violations of the honor code).

Cognitive-Psychological outcomes could include writing; speaking; critical thinking; and knowledge of specific content covered in the seminar, such as wellness topics, campus policies, school history, or a specific disciplinary topic.

While these outcomes provide a general idea of what can be assessed, each program will assess the specific learning outcomes they have established. The next section will address how to create learning outcomes that are well articulated, measurable, and relevant.

Writing Good Learning Outcomes

There is often confusion about the difference between goals and outcomes. Outcomes are different than goals in that they are more specific and measurable. As Figure 2.3 suggests, outcomes are often organized under goals. For instance, an institution may have a goal to "foster academic success." To measure this goal, however, a more precise definition of academic success is needed. For instance, one outcome among the many that perhaps collectively define academic success is the ability to apply appropriate academic strategies to courses and learning experiences. This outcome can be measured, providing an indicator of the extent to which the goal has been achieved.

Maki (2004) defined a learning outcome as a statement that "identifies what students should be able to *demonstrate* or *represent* or *produce* as a result of what and how they have learned in your course" (p. 61). In addition to helping clarify what should be assessed, learning outcomes are important because they focus the course by clearly defining intended objectives and

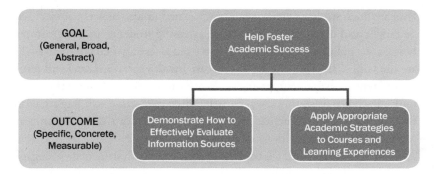

Figure 2.3. Distinguishing between goals and outcomes.

purpose (beginning with the end in mind) and shift the focus from teaching (i.e., what the instructor will do) to learning (i.e., what students will be able to do). Moreover, learning outcomes guide curriculum design, helping instructors determine what to teach, how to teach it, and when it should be taught. As such, the language used to define learning is very important because specific words will drive the assessment process in varying directions.

A helpful framework in developing a learning outcome is to ask, How will I know it when I see it? Thus, as Maki (2004) suggested, good outcomes must be observable. They should represent what students will be able to *do* as a result of the seminar. A useful stem to start this list of learning outcomes is the following: As a result of this course, students should_____. Maki also noted outcomes are focused on the end result, not the activities or methods designed to achieve the outcome. For example, it is not enough to say that 200 people attended a stress management workshop; rather, it is more useful to measure the extent to which the intended learning outcomes of that workshop were achieved by those participants. Therefore, good learning outcomes should avoid words that represent the environment or treatment, such as *experience*, *participate*, and *attend*.

A learning outcome will have a subject, verb, and object. For instance, consider the following outcome:

Students will be able to describe appropriate campus resources.

The subject is the *students*. The verb is *describe* and the object is *appropriate campus resources*. Selecting the correct verb is essential to both the curriculum design process and the assessment process. The verb will dictate not only the level at which students are expected to operate but also how the subject will be taught and measured. For example, assessing students' recall of campus honor code policies is markedly different from assessing their ability to evaluate the policy. The verb chosen in this case (*recall* versus *evaluate*) will result in different measurement strategies. *Recall* can be assessed easily through a multiple-choice or short-answer format, while *evaluation* will require more thoughtful strategies, such as an essay, a case study, or similar assignment requiring students to demonstrate their thinking.

The verb also reflects the cognitive process in which students will engage. In revising Bloom's Taxonomy, Anderson and Krathwohl (2001) arranged the cognitive processes on a continuum of increasing complexity, as follows: remembering, understanding, applying, analyzing, evaluating, and creating. While Bloom's Taxonomy is frequently depicted as a hierarchy, the cognitive processes are not intended to be cumulative, where one has to be accomplished before the next is possible (Anderson, 2005). Figure 2.4 provides examples of relevant verbs for each cognitive process.

Levels of cognitive process	Action verbs
Remembering *Can the student recall or remember the information?*	Define, duplicate, list, memorize, recall, repeat, reproduce, state
Understanding *Can the student explain ideas or concepts?*	Classify, describe, discuss, explain, identify, locate, recognize, report, select, translate, paraphrase
Applying *Can the student use the information in a new way?*	Choose, dramatize, demonstrate, employ, illustrate, interpret, operate, schedule, sketch, solve, use, write
Analyzing *Can the student distinguish between the different parts?*	Appraise, argue, compare, criticize, differentiate, discriminate, distinguish, examine, experiment, question, test
Evaluating *Can the student justify a position or decision?*	Appraise, argue, judge, defend, select, support, value, evaluate
Creating *Can the student create a new product or point of view?*	Assemble, construct, create, design, develop, formulate, write

Figure 2.4. Action verbs associated with cognitive processes in Bloom's Revised Taxonomy. (Adapted from Anderson & Krathwohl, 2001, p. 31). Reprinted from J. Gahagan, J. Dingfelder, and K. Pei, 2010, *A Faculty and Staff Guide to Creating Learning Outcomes*, p. 16. Copyright 2011 by the University of South Carolina.

The object is the type of knowledge addressed in the course. Anderson and Krathwohl (2001) added a knowledge dimension to Bloom's original taxonomy that is useful when determining what type of knowledge to assess as the object of the learning outcome. The four types of knowledge are (a) factual, (b) conceptual, (c) procedural, and (d) metacognitive. Anderson (2005) summarized each type.

» *Factual knowledge* includes elements that students must know to understand the subject matter, including terminology and details.
» *Conceptual knowledge* comprises classifications and categories; principles and generalizations; and theories, models, and structures. It also covers understanding the interrelationships among the basic elements within a larger structure that enable the elements to function together.
» *Procedural knowledge* (i.e., knowing how) involves the capacity to make or do something. It includes methods, techniques, algorithms, and skills.
» *Metacognitive knowledge* encompasses awareness of cognition in general and of one's own cognition in particular. It includes strategic knowledge, task knowledge, and self-knowledge.

While it may seem obvious, it is also important that the learning outcomes are achievable. They should be appropriate to the developmental level of students and the time frame and scope of the course. For instance, including 20 learning outcomes in a one-credit course may not be feasible because there is not adequate time to address all of them. In addition, asking first-year students to demonstrate high levels of metacognition or multicultural competence may not be realistic due to their developmental state. Developmental theories, such as Perry's or Baxter Magolda's work on cognitive development, Kohlberg's thoughts on moral reasoning, and Chickering's ideas about psychosocial development, are useful to determine the appropriate markers and milestones that are reasonable for first-year students to meet (Evans, Forney, & Guido-DiBrito, 1998; Skipper, 2005). In sum, the outcomes need to be consistent with what is reasonably possible to accomplish. More information on learning outcomes from diverse seminar types can be found in "Examples of Learning Outcomes" on pp. 22-24.

Examples of Learning Outcomes

University 101 at the University of South Carolina

Three-credit hour, extended-orientation course at a large, research university

Goal I. Foster Academic Success

As a result of this course, students will

» Adapt and apply appropriate academic strategies to their courses and learning experiences
» Demonstrate how to effectively evaluate information sources and utilize University libraries and information systems for academic inquiry
» Recognize the purpose and value of academic integrity and describe the key themes related to the Honor Code at the University of South Carolina
» Use written and oral communication to discover, develop, and articulate ideas and viewpoints
» Identify and apply strategies to effectively manage time and priorities
» Identify relevant academic polices, processes, and procedures related to advising, course planning, and major exploration

Goal II. Help Students Discover and Connect With the University of South Carolina

As a result of this course, students will

» Identify appropriate campus resources and opportunities that contribute to their educational experience, goals, and campus engagement
» Develop and apply skills that contribute to building positive relationships with peers, staff, and faculty
» Describe what it means to be a Carolinian in context of the history, traditions, and culture of the University

Goal III. Prepare Students for Responsible Lives in a Diverse, Interconnected, and Changing World

As a result of this course, students will

» Examine how their background and experiences impact their values and assumptions and explain the influence these have on their relationships with others

» Describe concepts of diversity and recognize diverse perspectives
» Describe and demonstrate principles of responsible citizenship within and beyond the campus community
» Describe processes, strategies, and resources, and explain the implications of their decisions, related to their overall wellness

Appalachian State University

Three-credit, academic seminar that is required as part of the general education curriculum at a public, masters-granting university

Goal: Thinking Critically and Creatively

» Recognize, differentiate, and effectively employ appropriate and increasingly sophisticated strategies to collect and interpret information
» Successfully integrate disparate concepts and information when interpreting, solving problems, evaluating, creating, and making decisions
» Examine and evaluate how personal, historical, and cultural perspectives affect the discovery and generation of knowledge

Goal: Communicating Effectively

» Articulate and comprehend effectively, using verbal or nonverbal communication suitable to topic, purpose, and audience
» Use writing effectively to discover and develop ideas and to articulate positions in contexts of increasing complexity

Goal: Understanding Responsibilities of Community Membership

» Collaborate effectively with others in shared processes of inquiry and problem solving

Elon University

Private college with three-credit, extended-orientation course

Students should be able to

» Articulate the purpose of the Elon Honor code and its significance to maintaining a vibrant community
» Communicate the basic fundamentals of the first-year core and general studies requirements
» Use basic advising planning tools
» Articulate the underlying importance of a basic liberal arts foundation to complement major requirements
» Identify basic campus resources to support their academic activities
» Locate and evaluate opportunities for campus-related involvement
» Communicate with their academic advisor about preregistration, academic requirements, and social issues or concerns.

Nash Community College

Public, two-year institution with one-hour, academic skills course

Students will

» Demonstrate effective note-taking skills
» Define and explain strategies for effective studying
» Identify and describe test-taking strategies
» Locate and use academic tutorial services
» Access and use a campus course management system, such as Blackboard or CampusCruiser
» Develop a semester-by-semester plan of study for degree completion

Conclusion

It is important to stress that assessment, in general, and the creation of learning outcomes, in particular, are not intended to be reductive exercises. Many faculty are concerned that assessment will lead to teaching only things that can be easily measured. While some outcomes are easier to measure than others, programs and departments should not discount a goal or outcome based on the difficulty of measurement. As Walvoord (2004) noted,

> Assessment does not limit itself to only learning that can be objectively tested. It need not be a reductive exercise. Rather, a department can state its highest goals, including goals such as students' ethical development, understanding of diversity, and the like. Then it can seek the best available indicators about whether those goals are being met (p. 2).

Learning outcomes simply articulate what students should be getting out of a course and then suggest reasonable measures for knowing whether or not students "got it." Once outcomes have been established, the next step in the assessment process is to design the appropriate educational approaches and curricula to achieve them. Then, faculty need to be developed and supported in their efforts toward these ends. Other volumes in this series on first-year seminars cover the issues of educational approaches to first-year seminars (Volume III by Garner, 2012) and recommendations about faculty development (Volume II by Groccia & Hunter, 2012). For the purpose of this volume on assessment, the next step in the process is to collect evidence.

Chapter 3
Approaches to Data Collection: The How of Assessment Planning

Once outcomes have been explicitly stated, the next step in the assessment process is to collect information. The key question is to determine what evidence is necessary to sufficiently infer that a student has met or achieved a specific outcome. Determining the types of data to collect and understanding the best ways to gather them can be the most vexing part of the assessment process. Other confusing points often include understanding the difference between a direct and indirect measure and whether quantitative or qualitative measures will yield more useful or meaningful results. This chapter will provide guidance on these issues, offering an overview of some commercially available assessment measures and guidance on developing local instruments (e.g., surveys, rubrics). A direct assessment of an information literacy outcome is provided as an example.

Collecting Data—Direct and Indirect Measures

There are two general methods by which data can be collected: direct and indirect. A *direct measure* provides tangible evidence about a student's knowledge, skill, or behavior, while an *indirect measure* is a student report of what he or she has gained, learned, or experienced. Palomba and Banta (1999) noted that "indirect measures ask students to reflect on their learning, rather than demonstrate it" (p. 12). As such, indirect measures often serve as proxies for measures of actual learning.

Indirect Measures

Several national instruments provide useful indirect measures of student learning relevant to a first-year seminar; however, the First-Year Initiative Assessment (FYI) is the only instrument designed specifically to assess first-year seminars. Factors on the FYI include academic and cognitive strategies, study strategies, knowledge of wellness, management of time and priorities, knowledge of campus policies, knowledge of academic services, critical thinking, connections with faculty, connections with peers, usefulness of course readings, engaging pedagogies, and overall course effectiveness. Custom reports can be generated to analyze the factors that best predict or explain overall course effectiveness. This report allows seminar leaders to learn not only how well the seminar performs in a given area, but how important that area is to the overall success of the course. In addition, data are broken down by demographic variables (i.e., SAT score, gender, race) to help determine how different populations perceive and benefit from the course. Individual reports can also be created for instructors comparing their scores with the means from all sections of the seminar at their institution.

Other instruments can be used to compare responses on items between participants in the seminar and nonparticipants. These instruments do not ask specifically about the impact of the seminar, but they do measure outcomes often associated with first-year seminars. A brief description of these instruments and their potential areas of focus relevant to assessing first-year seminars are provided below.

» *National Survey of Student Engagement (NSSE)* is a benchmarking instrument that assesses the level of student engagement on five factors: (a) academic challenge, (b) active and collaborative learning, (c) student-faculty interaction, (d) enriching educational experiences, and (e) supportive campus environment. The instrument includes a few individual items that measure the extent to which the experience at the institution contributed to knowledge, skills, and development in certain areas, including writing; speaking; critical thinking; learning effectively; understanding self; and solving complex, real-world problems. This instrument is administered to first-year students and seniors. It can be paired with the Beginning College Survey of Student Engagement (BCSSE) to show change over time.

» *Community College Survey of Student Engagement (CCSSE)* is a modified version of the NSSE that reflects the special mission, population, and realities of two-year institutions. The CCSSE and NSSE share an empirical research base on effective practices, and there is substantial overlap in the content of the surveys. The major difference is the omission of items inappropriate for two-year schools and the addition of items related to technical education, student support, and retention.

» *Your First College Year (YFCY)* serves as a follow up to the Freshman Survey, allowing for value-added research on the first year of college. The instrument also provides data on student outcomes and the educational environment relevant to the first year. Administered to new students at the end of the first year, this instrument assesses academic experiences in the first year of college, adjustment and transitions issues, student interactions, how students spend their time, and student values and goals.

» *College Outcomes Survey.* This instrument, published by ACT, assesses students' perceptions of the importance of, progress toward, and college contribution to, a variety of college outcomes, such as writing, speaking, critical thinking, diversity, study habits, and leadership. It also assesses satisfaction with selected aspects of the institution's programs and services.

» *College Student Experiences Questionnaire (CSEQ)* measures student quality of effort toward campus resources and opportunities for learning and development, student opinions about the priorities and emphases of the campus environment, and student self-reported progress toward a diverse range of educational outcomes.

» *College Student Survey (CSS).* Designed as an exit survey for graduating seniors, this instrument assesses an array of college outcomes and postcollege goals and plans including academic achievement and engagement, student-faculty interaction, cognitive and affective development, and satisfaction with the college experience.

» *Emotional Quotient Inventory (EQ-i)* examines an individual's social and emotional strengths and weaknesses. Scales include intrapersonal (e.g., assertiveness, independence), interpersonal (e.g., empathy, social responsibility), stress management, adaptability, and general mood (e.g., optimism, happiness).

» *Learning and Study Strategies Inventory (LASSI)* measures learning, study practices, and attitudes. Scales include attitude, motivation, time management, anxiety, concentration, information processing, study aids, self-testing, and test strategies. This instrument can be used as pretest, posttest, or both.

» *Student Adaptation to College Questionnaire (SACQ)* assesses adjustment to college in four areas, including academic, personal-emotional, social, and attachment to institution. The instrument is often used primarily as a screening tool for incoming students.

» *Student Development Task and Lifestyle Assessment (SDTLA)*
measures college students' psychosocial development. Four developmental
tasks measured include establishing and clarifying purpose, developing
autonomy, mature interpersonal relationships, and salubrious lifestyle.
This instrument can be used as both a pre- and posttest.

Appendix A provides an assessment plan that suggests how questions from
some of these surveys can be used to indirectly measure outcomes related to
a first-year seminar. For a more comprehensive list of available instruments,
visit the Measuring Quality in Higher Education Resource provided by the
Association of Institutional Research (http://applications.airweb.org/surveys).

Choosing Between Locally Developed and National Instruments

While a number of instruments are available that can be used to provide
indirect measures of student learning, locally developed instruments are also a
viable option. Ory (1994) suggested six factors to consider when determining
whether to develop a local instrument or to use an existing national instrument. These include (a) the purpose of the assessment; (b) the match between
the instrument and the intended outcomes; (c) logistical issues including cost,
time, and expertise; (d) the likely perception and acceptance of the instrument
at the institution; (e) the level of quality necessary; and (f) the motivation and
incentives for students to participate. Figure 3.1 provides a comparison of
commercial versus local instruments on these six factors.

The strengths of national instruments are that they can provide valuable
benchmarking comparisons, have established reliability and validity, have
greater perceived legitimacy, and can save substantial time and energy. While
locally developed instruments may lack the established reliability and validity of commercial instruments, they will be more aligned to the institution
or program's learning outcomes. For this reason, local instruments may enjoy
greater buy-in, as they are perceived to measure what is important to faculty
and to be more closely aligned with the needs and realities of a particular
campus (Suskie, 2004).

When designing a local survey or course assessment, program administrators should keep the following guidelines drawn from the work of Patten
(1998) and Cuseo (2001) in mind:

» Questions should be brief, clear, and simple.
» Rating scales that provide five to seven choice points or response options
are most useful. Cuseo noted that "fewer than five choices reduces the

instrument's ability to discriminate between satisfied and dissatisfied respondents, and more than seven rating-scale options adds nothing to the instrument's discriminability" (p. 67).

» Response options should be mutually exclusive. If, for example, respondents are asked to comment on how much time they spend using e-mail each week, the following response options are problematic:

☐ Never use ☐ < 1 hour ☐ 1-2 hours ☐ 2-3 hours ☐ > 3 hours

The responses below are better because now all the options are discrete choices:

☐ Never use ☐ < 1 hour ☐ 1-2 hours ☐ 3-4 hours ☐ > 4 hours

» Response options should strive to accurately capture the student experience by including a range of choices beyond agree or disagree. Rather than asking respondents their level agreement (i.e., strongly agree to strongly disagree) with the statement *I am satisfied with dining services*, having them rate their satisfaction (i.e., very satisfied to very dissatisfied) with dining services may yield more accurate information about student perceptions.

» Compound or double-barreled prompts, such as *The program was stimulating and useful*, ask the student to rate two different aspects of the program simultaneously. Because it is impossible to determine which aspect the respondent is rating, such prompts should be avoided.

» Providing a space beneath each question for comments may yield valuable additional information. As Cuseo noted, written comments often clarify or illuminate numerical ratings and are most useful for program and course improvement purposes.

» Including one or two negatively worded items requires students to reverse the rating scale (e.g., I did *not* receive useful information in this program.). Cuseo suggested that these items serve two purposes. First, they encourage the survey taker to be careful in reading and rating each item, and second, they could be used to identify the forms where a student may have simply rated all items either universally high or low rather than giving each item an individual evaluation.

» Clustering individual items comprising the program-evaluation instrument into categories that represent important program objectives or components serves as a signal to survey takers that there are distinct dimensions to the program, which makes it more likely that they will assess

Factor	Locally developed	Commerically available
Purpose	Allows thorough diagnostic coverage of local goals and content	Allows for comparison to national norm group
Match	Tailored to local goals and content	Usually provides incomplete coverage of local goals and content
Logistics		
Availability	Takes time and resources to develop	Only the purchase price is necessary
Prep Time	Considerable amount of time for instrument development	Can be obtained in short amount of time
Expertise	Takes content and measurement expertise to develop instrument	Can be administered and used after reading materials
Cost	Possibly expensive development costs	Purchasing, scoring, and reporting expenses
Scoring	Immediate	Can be delayed if scored off campus
Testing time	Flexible	Fixed
Test type	Built for local needs	Restricted to commercial availability
Ease in administration	Flexible	Requires standardized administration
Norms	Allows for intra-institutional comparison only	Allows for national and inter-institutional comparisons

Figure 3.1. Six-factor comparison of locally developed and commercially available assessment instruments. Adapted from "Suggestions for Deciding Between Commercially Available and Locally Developed Assessment Instruments," by J. Ory, 1994, *Evaluation Technical Assistance: Dissemination Series*, pp. 396-407. Copyright 1994 by J. Ory.

Factor	Locally developed	Commerically available
Reporting	Built for local needs	Restricted to commercial availability
Institutional acceptance	• Local development can encourage campus buy-in and acceptance • Quality concerns may interfere with acceptance	• Professional quality and national use may enhance acceptance • Failure to completely cover local goals and content may inhibit acceptance
Quality	Lack of professional quality may affect results and influence institutional acceptance	Professional quality may compensate for incomplete coverage of local goals and content
Student motivation	Local investment may not provide incentives for responding	Can provide incentives, such as a national comparison of practice for a future administration

them independently (Cuseo). This strategy may also reduce the risk of students carelessly completing the survey by filling in only 1s or 5s on all items, depending on whether they generally liked or disliked the program.

» Including at least two global items on the evaluation instrument provides insight into overall program effectiveness or impact. Such items may read, *I would recommend this course to others* or *Taking this course has been a valuable experience.* Careful thought should be given about where to place the global items in the survey. Putting them at the beginning of the instrument may yield a big-picture, gut-feeling response from participants. Placing the global items at the end of the instrument may yield a response that considers overall effectiveness in light of all the other survey items.

» Respondents should also be asked to provide written comments on the program's strengths and weaknesses along with suggestions about how the latter can be improved.

» Sensitive issues and questions that may be perceived as threatening are more likely to be answered if they are saved for the concluding portion when rapport is greatest.

» Demographic or biographic questions should be listed last. If some respondents decline to answer these, other data may still be usable.

Before distributing the survey to the sample or population, it is important to make sure the wording and formats are as clear as possible. One way to work through the kinks is to conduct a *think aloud*, where someone from outside the intended population or sample takes the survey and verbalizes his or her response to each question. Listening to the responses will help the survey designer determine whether the respondent is interpreting the question in the way it was intended. As such, a think aloud can help identify questions that are ambiguous or have inappropriate response choices (Patten, 1998).

Direct Measures

A direct measure is tangible evidence of a student's ability, performance, or experience. It can be an artifact of what students have learned or are able to do. Examples of direct measures include papers, oral presentations, journals, assignments, tests, and portfolios. Indirect measures are useful for gauging student satisfaction or providing stories and context to explain or illustrate findings. However, direct measures are generally more desirable because they provide actual evidence, not just perceptions or proxies for learning. For instance, if one outcome of a seminar is to foster better writing, it would be more powerful to compare a writing sample from early in the course to a later one for evidence of improvement than to ask students if, as a result of the course, they are better writers.

As with indirect measures, several commercial instruments are available that provide direct measures of student learning, knowledge, and abilities relevant to a first-year seminar. They provide evidence of students' knowledge or skills rather than just self-reported gains or measures of satisfaction. Below is a summary of several types of instruments.

Placement exams—such as Accuplacer (College Board), ASSET (ACT), and COMPASS (ACT)—which are used for diagnostic and placement purposes, can also provide baseline data about students' knowledge and skills. When paired with tests of general education, skills, and knowledge (described below), placement exams can measure change over time. Instruments assessing general education skills and knowledge include the following:

> » *ETS Proficiency Profile* assesses critical thinking, reading, writing, and mathematics across three areas of study, including humanities, social sciences, and natural sciences.

» *CollegeBASE* assesses knowledge of four subject areas (i.e., English, math, science, social studies) and provides performance rankings in higher order thinking skills (i.e., interpretive, strategic, and adaptive reasoning abilities)

» *Collegiate Assessment of Academic Proficiency (CAAP)* is usually given at end of sophomore year, but it can also be used to gather baseline data on incoming students. This instrument can be compared with scores on the COMPASS exam, a placement exam that provides baseline data about students' knowledge and skills, to indicate change over time.

Information literacy is emerging as a critical academic skill, and several instruments have been developed to assess students' knowledge and capabilities in this area. These include the ICT Literacy Assessment by the Educational Testing Service, Project SAILS (Standardized Assessment of Information Literacy) by Kent State University, and the Information Literacy Test by James Madison University.

The development of critical-thinking skills is a frequent objective of first-year seminars, especially among academic seminars (Padgett & Keup, 2011). Several national instruments provide measures of students' ability to think critically. Three prominent assessments include the following:

» *California Critical Thinking Skills Test* measures several dimensions of critical thinking, including analysis and interpretation, inferences, and evaluation and explanation.

» *Watson-Glaser Critical Thinking Appraisal* is generally used by businesses to make hiring and promotion decisions. It measures a person's ability to make accurate inferences, recognize assumptions, properly deduce, interpret information, and evaluate arguments.

» *Collegiate Learning Assessment (CLA)* measures critical thinking, writing, and problem solving. Unlike most other instruments, the CLA is a production task instrument, which requires students to construct a written response based on a set of artifacts, rather than simply recognize a correct answer. It is perhaps the most well-known of the critical-thinking tests because of the attention it received by the Secretary of Education's Commission on the Future of Higher Education and Arum and Roksa's work (2011).

Course-Embedded Assignments

Getting usable and accurate direct measures of student learning can be challenging. Motivation is a significant factor that must be addressed. Many institutions have experimented with Assessment Days where time is set aside by cancelling classes for students to engage in a battery of assessments, ranging from filling out surveys to writing essays, taking exams, or giving presentations. This strategy may be falling out of favor because institutions have learned that while they could put enough requirements in place to ensure students participated in the assessments (e.g., not allowing students to register for courses), without the proper carrot, they could not ensure students would put forth their best efforts. Students realized that there was no penalty for not doing well; consequently, these institutions could not ensure that the results of the assessments were reflective of the students' best efforts.

So, how does an institution ensure its students take assessment seriously? The best way may be to embed the assessment into existing courses so that students are rewarded with academic credit and a grade. This assessment does not require students to do anything extra or different; therefore, it provides an authentic measure of learning as demonstrated in regular class activities. Embedding the assessment in the workload of the seminar also ensures that students both participate in the assessment and take it seriously (at least as seriously as they take their grades).

While every student will be completing an assignment, not every assignment needs to be programmatically assessed. Students could be asked to submit the best representations of evidence of their learning, and a random sample of documents could be evaluated to analyze multiple outcomes, such as critical thinking, writing, adjustment to college, or time management.

For instance, information literacy can be assessed by applying a rubric to a research paper. A rubric is a scoring guide describing the criteria that will be used to evaluate an assignment. It identifies the important traits and describes the levels of performance (e.g., unacceptable to excellent) within each of the traits. If the rubric is broad enough in scope, it may be appropriate to use a single guide for various types of research assignments.

Suskie (2004) identified four types of rubrics. The first are *checklists*, which would be used to indicate whether a trait was present. For example, a checklist item for a research project might read, "sources were appropriately documented." The second type of rubric is a *rating scale*, which provides a range of responses to each trait, such as *strongly agree* to *strongly disagree* or a *great extent* to *not at all*. Figure 3.2 provides an example of a rating scale rubric.

	Strongly agree	Agree	Disagree	Strongly disagree
The introduction was effective.	☐	☐	☐	☐
The presentation was organized in a logical manner.	☐	☐	☐	☐
The presentation included smooth transitions.	☐	☐	☐	☐
Delivery was effective (i.e., consider eye contact, avoiding "umms" and "like," reading directly from notes, tone, gestures, pace, posture).	☐	☐	☐	☐
The presentation was engaging.	☐	☐	☐	☐
The speaker seemed prepared.	☐	☐	☐	☐
The topic was well-researched and documented appropriately.	☐	☐	☐	☐
The information presented was relevant to the topic.	☐	☐	☐	☐
The PowerPoint was well designed (i.e., consider color schemes, layout, graphics, font, use of keywords, acknowledging sources on each slide).	☐	☐	☐	☐
The conclusion was effective.	☐	☐	☐	☐

Figure 3.2. A rating scale rubric for an oral presentation.

A third type of rubric is *descriptive*. Rather than use checkboxes to indicate the level of achievement, these scoring guides provide a description of what the rating means. The Association of American Colleges and Universities (AAC&U) has created numerous assessment rubrics for general education related outcomes, including writing, critical thinking, and information literacy. The AAC&U Rubric on Information Literacy (Rhodes, 2010) offers a good example of a descriptive rubric (Figure 3.3).

This type of rubric helps ensure a higher degree of interrater reliability because the ratings are more defined and less open to subjective interpretation than other types of rubrics. Yet, a cautionary note is necessary here. Griffin (2009) suggested that while rubrics have evolved into technically precise documents, their air of certainty is deceptive since rubrics are a reflection of the people who designed them rather than "permanent or absolute reality" (p.4). Thus, what may seem to be an objective and precise evaluation of a student's ability is in reality still very much just a way of organizing the subjectivity inherent in evaluating student work.

The fourth type of scoring guide identified by Suskie (2004) is a *holistic rubric*. Rather than list the traits that are being assessed, this rubric provides a short narrative of the characteristics of work at varying levels of performance (see Figure 3.4). Holistic rubrics are designed to be a bit more generic so they can be applied across a wider variety of work. This can be very useful in assessing first-year seminars with variable content.

As with the selection of a survey instrument, program leaders must choose between finding an existing rubric and creating a customized version. Developing a rubric locally would ensure that what the program and institution truly value is being measured. To get started, program leaders should consider what success looks like for the particular outcome. It might be helpful to gather a few key individuals to think through these questions. Having faculty develop rubrics, particularly to apply to existing course assignments, is a great way to reiterate the purpose and intended outcomes of the seminar and of specific assignments. It reminds faculty of what they are trying to accomplish and gives some further refinement to the characteristics of the work students are expected to demonstrate in the assignment. Appendix B offers a sample first-year assessment plan incorporating course-embedded assessments and a locally developed rubric.

For more information on rubrics, readers can consult *Assessing Student Learning* by Suskie (2004) and Walvoord and Anderson's (1998) *Effective Grading*. In addition, the Office of Academic Assessment at the University of

INFORMATION LITERACY VALUE RUBRIC

for more information, please contact value@aacu.org

The VALUE rubrics were developed by teams of faculty experts representing colleges and universities across the United States through a process that examined many existing campus rubrics and related documents for each learning outcome and incorporated additional feedback from faculty. The rubrics articulate fundamental criteria for each learning outcome, with performance descriptors demonstrating progressively more sophisticated levels of attainment. The rubrics are intended for institutional-level use in evaluating and discussing student learning, not for grading. The core expectations articulated in all 15 of the VALUE rubrics can and should be translated into the language of individual campuses, disciplines, and even courses. The utility of the VALUE rubrics is to position learning at all undergraduate levels within a basic framework of expectations such that evidence of learning can by shared nationally through a common dialog and understanding of student success.

Definition

The ability to know when there is a need for information, to be able to identify, locate, evaluate, and effectively and responsibly use and share that information for the problem at hand. -Adopted from the National Forum on Information Literacy

Framing Language

This rubric is recommended for use evaluating a collection of work, rather than a single work sample in order to fully gauge students' information skills. Ideally, a collection of work would contain a wide variety of different types of work and might include: research papers, editorials, speeches, grant proposals, marketing or business plans, PowerPoint presentations, posters, literature reviews, position papers, and argument critiques to name a few. In addition, a description of the assignments with the instructions that initiated the student work would be vital in providing the complete context for the work. Although a student's final work must stand on its own, evidence of a student's research and information gathering processes, such as a research journal/diary, could provide further demonstration of a student's information proficiency and for some criteria on this rubric would be required.

Figure 3.3. AAC&U rubric on information literacy. Reprinted with permission from *Assessing Outcomes and Improving Achievement: Tips and Tools for Using Rubrics,* edited by Terrel L. Rhodes. Copyright 2010 by the Association of American Colleges and Universities.

Figure 3.3 continues, p.40.

Figure 3.3 continues.

INFORMATION LITERACY VALUE RUBRIC

for more information, please contact value@aacu.org

Definition

The ability to know when there is a need for information, to be able to identify, locate, evaluate, and effectively and responsibly use and share that information for the problem at hand. - The National Forum on Information Literacy

Evaluators are encouraged to assign a zero to any work sample or collection of work that does not meet benchmark (cell one) level performance.

	Capstone 4	Milestones 2	Milestones 3	Benchmark 1
Determine the Extent of Information Needed	Effectively defines the scope of the research question or thesis. Effectively determines key concepts. Types of information (sources) selected directly relate to concepts or answer research question.	Defines the scope of the research question or thesis completely. Can determine key concepts. Types of information (sources) selected relate to concepts or answer research question.	Defines the scope of the research question or thesis incompletely (parts are missing, remains too broad or too narrow, etc.). Can determine key concepts. Types of information (sources) selected partially relate to concepts or answer research question.	Has difficulty defining the scope of the research question or thesis. Has difficulty determining key concepts. Types of information (sources) selected do not relate to concepts or answer research question.
Access the Needed Information	Accesses information using effective, well-designed search strategies and most appropriate information sources.	Accesses information using variety of search strategies and some relevant information sources. Demonstrates ability to refine search.	Accesses information using simple search strategies, retrieves information from limited and similar sources.	Accesses information randomly, retrieves information that lacks relevance and quality.

Evaluate Information and its Sources Critically	Thoroughly (systematically and methodically) analyzes own and others' assumptions and carefully evaluates the relevance of contexts when presenting a position.	Identifies own and others' assumptions and several relevant contexts when presenting a position.	Questions some assumptions. Identifies several relevant contexts when presenting a position. May be more aware of others' assumptions than one's own (or vice versa).	Shows an emerging awareness of present assumptions (sometimes labels assertions as assumptions). Begins to identify some contexts when presenting a position.
Use Information Effectively to Accomplish a Specific Purpose	Communicates, organizes and synthesizes information from sources to fully achieve a specific purpose, with clarity and depth.	Communicates, organizes, and synthesizes information from sources. Intended purpose is achieved.	Communicates and organizes information from sources. The information is not yet synthesized, so the intended purpose is not fully achieved.	Communicates information from sources. The information is fragmented and/or used inappropriately (misquoted, taken out of context, or incorrectly paraphrased, etc.), so the intended purpose is not achieved.
Access and Use Information Ethically and Legally	Students use correctly all of the following information use strategies (use of citations and references; choice of paraphrasing, summary, or quoting; using information in ways that are true to original context; distinguishing between common knowledge and ideas requiring attribution) and demonstrate a full understanding of the ethical and legal restrictions on the use of published, confidential, and/or proprietary information.	Students use correctly three of the following information use strategies (use of citations and references; choice of paraphrasing, summary, or quoting; using information in ways that are true to original context; distinguishing between common knowledge and ideas requiring attribution) and demonstrate a full understanding of the ethical and legal restrictions on the use of published, confidential, and/or proprietary information.	Students use correctly two of the following information use strategies (use of citations and references; choice of paraphrasing, summary, or quoting; using information in ways that are true to original context; distinguishing between common knowledge and ideas requiring attribution and demonstrate a full understanding of the ethical and legal restrictions on the use of published, confidential, and/or proprietary information.	Students use correctly one of the following information use strategies (use of citations and references; choice of paraphrasing, summary, or quoting; using information in ways that are true to original context; distinguishing between common knowledge and ideas requiring attribution) and demonstrate a full understanding of the ethical and legal restrictions on the use of published, confidential, and/or proprietary information.

The A Paper

The A paper has a central theme expressed explicitly in the thesis statement and developed consistently through the paper. It is easy to follow because it is logically developed and written clearly. Each paragraph has focus, unity, and coherence. There is smooth transition between sentences and paragraphs. Assertions are supported by examples. Words and ideas are used precisely. The paper is free of mechanical errors, is interesting to read, and shows imagination. The conclusion does not merely restate the thesis, but summarizes the entire paper in order to make the reader understand the subject on a higher level.

The B Paper

The B paper has a clearly and succinctly written thesis sentence. It is easy to follow, and its paragraphs have focus and unity. It may lack coherence and smooth transition at some points and have one or two mechanical errors. But each paragraph is well-developed, and the conclusion summarizes the entire paper.

The B- or C+ Paper

The B- or C+ paper has a clearly stated purpose, is somewhat logical, and is almost adequately developed. It presents examples after assertions, has unity, but its paragraphs might lack focus and coherence. It may contain a few sentences that need transposing, and it may have mechanical errors and errors in grammar, but it should indicate a level of competence.

The C Paper

The C paper's thesis may be too wordy though it may be clearly stated. It contains a few mechanical and grammatical errors, and it lacks liveliness of expression. It has problems with focus, development, and transition. Its conclusion reveals little more than a superficial understanding of the subject.

The C- or D+ Paper

The C- or D+ paper has a central idea organized enough to convey its purpose to the reader. It may be without vigor of thought and expression and may contain many errors in the use of English. These errors may be sentence fragments, spelling, verb-tense shifts, lack of "ed" or "s" verb endings, a confusion of the use of "there" and "it" at the beginning of sentences, a confusion of noun and adjective word endings, etc. With more careful proofreading and fuller development, many C- or D+ papers might be worth at least a C rating.

Figure 3.4. Holistic scoring guide. Reprinted from *University 101 Faculty Resource Manual 2.0*, pp. 6-7. Copyright, 2012, University of South Carolina.

The D Paper
The D paper may contain two ideas either of which could serve the central theme. It lacks focus and unity, and it has serious mechanical errors. It lacks imagination.

The F Paper
The F paper has all of the problems of the D paper but to a greater degree. In addition to these problems, the F paper may also have numerous incoherent or illegible sentences, a preponderance of misspelled words, and errors in grammar. The F paper shows no evidence of focus, organization, or development.

North Carolina at Greensboro provides a useful website with sample rubrics for dozens of different fields and disciplines (http://assessment.uncg.edu/rubrics/). Another helpful resource is Rubistar, a website that allows teachers to create their own custom rubrics (http://rubistar.4teachers.org).

Assessing a learning outcome using direct measures can be very time consuming, especially compared with the relative ease of scoring indirect quantitative measures. Using only direct measures in an overall assessment plan is usually not a feasible strategy because of the time and personnel involved in the process. This approach might force an institution to focus only on one or two outcomes per year instead of assessing all outcomes. A more workable strategy would be to indirectly assess each learning outcome yearly and choose a handful of outcomes (one to two) to assess directly each year. Blaich and Wise (2011) strongly encouraged institutions to focus their plans on one outcome, but no more than two or three, noting "in our experience, institutions that try to engage in too many initiatives wind up accomplishing none of them" (p. 13). When trying to identify which outcomes to assess first, several questions can guide decision making.

» *What matters most to the overall course effectiveness?* Is there any information that correlates a certain outcome with the overall effectiveness of the seminar? For example, the First-Year Initiative Assessment provides an analysis of the factors that most strongly predict students' perceptions of overall course effectiveness. Programs may choose to focus assessment efforts on factors identified that closely align with the content and learning outcomes of their curriculum that matter most to course effectiveness.

» *What matters most to persistence and grades?* Is there an outcome that most closely predicts student success? This could be answered by prior research on the campus level or through the theoretical literature base.

» *Which outcomes would position the seminar well politically?* Which outcomes, if successful, would strengthen the case for providing greater resources, including it in the general education curriculum, or requiring the course of all students (if desired)? Which outcomes provide the most credibility and legitimacy for the course? This would vary by institution and type of seminar offered (e.g., extended orientation, academic themed, study skills). On some campuses, improving study strategies might not carry the same weight as increasing writing proficiency or strengthening information literacy skills.

» *What is doable?* All the learning outcomes should be measurable, but some are easier to assess than others. It might be wise to start with a more accessible outcome so that assessment efforts are established on a solid foundation.

For an example of a direct assessment in a first-year seminar, see "A Direct Measure of Information Literacy" on pp. 50-51.

Qualitative Assessment Methods

The foregoing discussion of indirect and direct measures has focused on quantitative methods. Yet, there may be certain questions or outcomes that are best viewed through a qualitative lens. While qualitative assessment or research cannot be used to make generalizations about a population, it can be used to clarify issues, explore questions, or interpret and explain findings. Patton (2002) noted that "understanding the program's and participants' stories is useful to the extent that they illuminate the processes and outcomes of the program for those who must make decisions about the program" (p. 10). It can help us better understand what the numbers mean by providing context, examples, and stories. As Patton suggested, "qualitative findings illuminate the people behind the numbers and put faces on the statistics, not to make hearts bleed, though that may occur, but to deepen understanding" (p. 10). Qualitative approaches are also useful to generate and refine quantitative research questions and methods. For instance, learning from a focus group that many students think the seminar is too rigorous as compared to other first-year courses might lead to surveying former students to see if this belief is more widely held.

Patton (2002) identified three major kinds of qualitative data: (a) observations, (b) documents, and (c) interviews and focus groups. These are described in greater detail below with respect to first-year seminar assessment.

Observations

Observational research serves to bring the reader into the lived setting, providing descriptive detail of what happened (Patton, 2002). These studies often involve fieldwork descriptions of activities, behaviors, and actions, based on observations during site visits and peer review sessions. While time consuming and difficult, direct observation can be used to paint a portrait of what is happening in the seminar. During a peer review session or site visit, the observer may describe the quality of instruction, explore classroom dynamics, identify elements of a successful seminar, and document the existence of a welcoming environment or collaborative learning. Peer leaders can also be trained to collect these data.

Documents

Documents are another source of data that can be examined and interpreted to provide an understanding of the impact of the first-year seminar. Lincoln and Guba (1985) suggested that documents are a potentially rich source of information because they are readily available and grounded in the context they represent. For the purpose of assessing a first-year seminar, relevant documents might include

» *Written responses to surveys or course evaluations.* These data provide a rich and deep understanding about the course that elucidate formative feedback about what works, what needs improvement, and how satisfied students are. Written responses can be mined for, and grouped by, themes.
» *Course syllabi.* These documents could be mined to explore how the course is communicated to students; implicit and explicit messages about the value and purpose of the seminar; the number, type, clarity, and rigor of assignments; or the general tone of classroom policies.
» *Student journals, letters, photographs, or other documents produced during the semester.* Documents of this type could be used to assess

adjustment and transition issues, satisfaction and engagement with the life of the institution, or other important topics.

» *Facebook, Twitter, or Rate My Professor posts about the course.* As with all qualitative assessment, care should be taken not to extrapolate meaning beyond the context or generalize to the larger population. However, these data could provide specific examples about how the course is perceived by various stakeholders. For instance, a review of instructors on Rate My Professor could help seminar administrators understand student perceptions of the level of rigor in the course and general satisfaction with the seminar and instructor. A hashtag search on Twitter for the course title and institution could yield information about stakeholder's thinking of and reaction to the course. But given the methodological limitations inherent in social media applications, these data should not be used for summative or evaluative purposes.

Interviews and Focus Groups

Interviews and focus groups use open-ended questions to "yield in-depth responses about people's experiences, perceptions, opinions, feelings, and knowledge" (Patton, 2002, p. 4). Patton (2002) noted, "we interview people to find out from them those things we cannot directly observe" (p. 340). In assessing a first-year seminar, interviews can be used to help determine what people think and to gather stories to better understand the impact and experience of the seminar. Individual interviews can be a powerful tool to discover what students or instructors (or any other stakeholder) think about the course, how it has impacted learning or transition, and how the experience might be improved for others. Interviews can be conducted with current first-year students enrolled in the course, former students, students who did not take the seminar, instructors, peer leaders, parents, and others.

Interviews vary by the level of structure, ranging from an informal conversation with no set questions to a structured interview with rigid, pre-defined questions that are asked of all participants. Lincoln and Guba (1985) suggested that structured interviews are useful when "the interviewer knows what he or she does not know" (p. 269) and knows what questions need to be answered. On the other hand, unstructured interviews are best in cases where the interviewer knows little about the topic and does not have a clear idea of possible areas to explore. For a thorough treatment of interview techniques and strategies, readers can consult Patton's (2002) work on qualitative methods.

A subcategory of interviews is focus groups. Growing out of consumer and market research methods, focus groups were designed to use the social context in which decisions are made (Patton, 2002). Focus groups, unlike individual interviews, allow participants to react to other people's comments and adjust their own thinking. Patton (2002) noted, "the object is to get high-quality data in a social context where people can consider their own views in the context of the views of others" (p. 386). As the name implies, focus groups are designed to explore a narrow (i.e., focused) topic. Rather than exploring all aspects of the seminar, focus groups could concentrate on a specific area of the course, such as the textbook, use of peer leaders, or level of workload and rigor.

Focus groups are also useful in interpreting information that has already been gathered (Palomba & Banta, 1999). For instance, if quantitative data suggest that course readings contribute strongly to the overall effectiveness of the course, a student focus group might help explain why readings play an important role in the overall success of the course or which types of reading are most effective.

Krueger and Casey (2009) provided a comprehensive guide on designing and implementing focus groups. Their recommendations include the following:

» To keep the discussion manageable, the optimal size for a focus group is 6-10 participants. In order to yield a group that size, those charged with assessment may need to invite 15-20 individuals.
» Group members should possess similar characteristics in ways that are important to the research questions (Krueger & Casey, 2009). For the sake of assessing first-year seminars, the common characteristic would be participation in the seminar. However, if an institution offers seminars for distinct and varied populations, or if the requirements vary based on the type of seminar, it might be wise to conduct different focus groups for these populations. For instance, if one group of students is required to take the seminar and others are not, joining them together could make the interpretation of findings more difficult. As such, it would be prudent to separate the groups.
» Group members should not know each other. If members of the group know each other outside the focus group context, they may not be completely open and honest in their remarks (Bernard, 2002; Krueger & Casey, 2009).

» It is generally recommended that the focus group discussion last between 60 and 90 minutes. In that time frame, there is time for approximately five to seven questions, including follow-up and probing questions.

» Running a focus group generally requires both a moderator and a note taker. The moderator's task is to facilitate the process, ask probing and follow-up questions, and make sure all voices are being heard. This should be someone who is not known to the participants and who would not influence the responses of the group (Bernard, 2002; Krueger & Casey, 2009). Further, the moderator needs to avoid being judgmental or defensive. As such, special consideration must be given when selecting the moderator.

A variation on the focus group that has been used at several institutions is a student advisory council or similar group. The University of South Carolina uses a Student Advisory Council (SAC) to provide ongoing feedback about the first-year seminar. Rather than meeting one time (as with a focus group), the SAC meets regularly throughout the fall semester. Course sections are identified through a stratified random sample (to ensure many different section types are represented), and the students in each selected section are asked to elect one representative to serve on the council. To maintain group homogeneity, students who are required to take the course are placed in a separate council from students who elect to take the class. Unlike a focus group, serving on the council is portrayed and perceived as an honor, so this makes it relatively easy to ensure ongoing student participation. Participants are informed that they represent the interests of their University 101 class and future University 101 students. This group is used to assess perceptions about course content, class activities, pedagogical methods, the role of the peer leader, the effectiveness of the textbook and other readings, and the overall expectations of the seminar. In addition, the group serves to explore and discuss the relevance of course outcomes, which is an important way to ensure the seminar is focusing on topics that students need to learn.

Conclusion

It is common to feel alone in the assessment process, but help is likely available on every campus. Resources, allies, and assistance can be found in Offices of Institutional Research, Division of Student Life or Affairs, and in relevant departments. For instance, many faculty members in education or psychology (or other social sciences) are well-versed in assessment and social science research and may be able to help design an assessment strategy and assist with the data analysis. Faculty members in disciplines related to the skill set being assessed can also be called on for support. For instance, in developing a plan to directly assess information literacy, the experts in the library and/or a college or school of library and information science would be invaluable.

A Direct Assessment Measure of Information Literacy

One course learning outcome of University 101 at the University of South Carolina is to demonstrate effective evaluation of information sources and use of University libraries and information systems for academic inquiry. To decide the best method to gather direct evidence of student's knowledge and skills related to information literacy, University 101 staff met with several campus partners, including the chair of the Department of Library and Information Sciences and staff from the University Library. Two viable options were considered: (a) developing a rubric to apply to existing research assignments in the course and (b) administering a pre- and posttest of students' knowledge related to how to find, retrieve, and evaluate information sources. Because University 101 does not require any common research assignments, developing a standard rubric was not feasible. Thus, the pre- and posttest was selected as the main avenue to assess information literacy.

Several national instruments seemed relevant to our assessment needs, including tests from Educational Testing Service, ProjectSAILS (Standardized Assessment of Information Literacy Skills) at Kent State University, and the Center for Assessment and Research Studies at James Madison University. The advantages of these instruments were that they had already developed the questions and methodology and had established reliability and validity, thus saving time and ensuring a high-quality assessment. However, these tests measured more than the University 101 program cared to assess, making the instrument longer than necessary for our purposes. Since it was decided to administer the tests in class, it was necessary to ensure that the instrument would not take more than 20-25 minutes to complete. Another major concern was cost. Thus, the decision was made to create our own instrument.

With help from the library faculty, an 18-item test was developed. Questions were based on standards set by the Association of College and Research Libraries and focused on five categories of skills: (a) selecting search tools, (b) developing search strategies, (c) retrieving information, (d) evaluating information, and (e) documenting sources found. Prior to administering the test, several think alouds were conducted with students to ensure the questions were clearly and accurately worded. After several revisions, the pretest was ready to be administered. Each University 101 instructor was notified via e-mail about the project and what would be assessed, why, how, and when. The announcement also noted that while a random sample of course sections would be selected, all instructors were being made aware of how the information literacy learning outcome would be measured. It was hoped this communiqué would strengthen efforts to achieve the outcome and further refine the aspects of information literacy that should be addressed in class.

A random sample of 27 class sections (out of 160 sections) was selected to participate in the assessment. The pretest was administered during the first two weeks of the fall 2010 semester and yielded 557 completed tests. The post-test was administered the last two weeks of the fall semester and yielded 478 completed results. After cleaning the data and merging the pre- and posttest datasets, 399 usable records remained for analysis. Data from an instructor survey that ascertained the types of strategies used to teach information literacy knowledge and skills were incorporated into the dataset. The main variables on the instructor survey were (a) Did the class attend an information literacy workshop at the library? and (b) Was the class required to complete an online information literacy tutorial?

Four main research questions were posed: (a) Based on the pretest, with which aspects of information literacy do students struggle the most when they first arrive on campus? (b) To what extent do UNIV 101 students improve their knowledge of information literacy over the course of the first semester? (c) Which aspects of information literacy do students improve on the most? and (d) To what extent did attending the library or doing the online tutorial impact the gains?

One concern with the posttest was whether students would take the appropriate effort to answer the questions carefully. The most effective way to ensure that students gave their best effort was to embed the assessment in the course assignments and grades. Thus, instructors were requested to count the results from the posttest as either one of the quiz grades or for extra credit.

Several versions of a report were written to share with the multiple audiences. Instructors were informed early in the semester about the results of the pretest so they could plan their lessons accordingly. In addition, results were shared and processed with the librarians to enable them to modify the library workshop accordingly. The posttest data were shared with a wide group of stakeholders, including instructors, librarians, administrators, and campus faculty. Implications of the data were discussed with a group of instructors and campus experts on information literacy and were used to revise approaches to covering this topic.

Chapter 4
Approaches to Data Collection:
The Who of Assessment Planning

The previous chapter addressed a range of measures and methods for collecting assessment data. As noted in chapter 1, the primary focus of this book is programmatic rather than individual assessment. Yet, in order for programmatic assessment to proceed, program administrators need completed surveys, course artifacts, interview or focus group transcripts, and so on. This chapter addresses questions related to participants in assessment. Specifically, sampling techniques and strategies for improving response rates are described. The chapter closes with a discussion of groups associated with the first-year seminar that might logically be the focus of assessment efforts.

Sampling Methods

A population is the entire group of interest. Yet, most data collection involves the use of sampling, which provides a method of gathering information without surveying all people in a population—for example, all students enrolled in the first-year seminar. If there are only a handful of sections, one could easily gather data from every student. Gathering data from an entire population is called a census. For larger programs, assessing every student is neither feasible nor necessary. In addition, even if the program has the ability to survey every student, sampling can be used to help minimize survey fatigue (Schuh, 2009), by reducing the number of surveys to which individual students are asked to respond. A well-chosen sample can provide the same quality of data as a census in a more manageable way.

There are many ways to gather a sample. The appropriate technique will depend on whether the findings need to be generalized back to the entire population of interest (i.e., probability sampling). Below are a few techniques for creating samples, some of which will allow findings to be generalized to a whole population.

Probability Sampling

» *Random sampling.* This is the most straightforward method of probability sampling. Participants are chosen at random from a list of the entire population, perhaps through a table of random numbers, by drawing names out of a hat, or by selecting every Nth name from a list. Random number generators, readily available on the Internet, are useful for selecting a random sample. Statistical programs, such as SPSS, and spreadsheets, such as EXCEL, also have random generator features.

» *Stratified sampling.* To minimize sampling errors, or to ensure that the sample includes an appropriate number of people with certain characteristics (e.g., gender, class standing, race or ethnicity), assessment professionals use stratified sampling. This technique is useful for making generalizations about subgroups. For instance, to ensure the sample is representative of the number of males and females who enroll in the seminar, the sample percentage should be equal to the percentage of the actual population. Thus, if 70% of the participants are females, the sample should be composed of 70% females and 30% males. If the seminar has sections for different types of populations (e.g., honors, first-generation, at risk, major specific), stratifying the sample may be more representative than a simple random sample. It is important to note that some subgroups are less likely to respond (e.g., men), so it might be beneficial to oversample these groups to ensure that the final number of responses reflects the actual population.

» *Cluster sampling.* Also used for making generalizations to a subgroup, this is a form of random sampling in which a series of random selections are made for units of progressively smaller sizes. When assessing first-year seminars, it is often impractical to conduct a simple random sample. That strategy might result in having to survey a handful of students from many different sections. If the assessment is to be administered in class, or if artifacts of learning are to be collected, it is often easier to randomly select course sections rather than students. This type of sampling is referred to as cluster sampling.

Nonprobability Sampling

Nonprobability samples are easier to gather but do not lend themselves to generalizing to a larger population. These are often useful for qualitative methods, which cannot be generalized anyway. There are many nonprobability methods, but two of the most popular include the following:

> » *Samples of convenience.* As the name implies, this type of sampling involves using participants who are accessible and willing.
> » *Snowball sampling.* This sampling design asks "previously identified group members to identify other members of the population" (Henry, 1990, p 21).

Sample Sizes

What is the right size for a sample? It depends on size of population, up to a point. Table 4.1 provides recommended sample sizes for different size populations. It is important to note that the maximum size of a sample necessary to generalize to any size population, assuming a 3% margin of error, is around 1,000. Major polls conducted by organizations such as Gallop that seek to generalize to the entire population of the United States often have samples of this size. Many people are incredulous when told that a sample of 1,000 can speak to a population of 300 million people. Alreck and Settle (1995) provided a useful analogy to understand how this concept is possible:

> Suppose you are warming a bowl of soup for yourself and you want to know if it's hot enough. You would probably sample it by stirring the soup, then trying a spoonful. The sample size would be one spoonful. Now assume you are to warm a hundred gallons of soup for a large crowd, and you want to test it to see if it's hot enough to serve. You would probably stir it and take a sample of one spoonful, even though the so-called population of the soup was hundreds of times larger than when only one serving was sampled. (p. 62)

The key to an effective sample is the degree to which it is representative of the people in the population. As Upcraft, Ishler, and Swing (2005) noted, "the representativeness of the sample is probably more important than the size of the sample. A small, useable sample, if it is representative of the population, is probably more credible than a large sample that is not representative" (p. 492). To be representative, the number of people within certain categories or demographics that complete the survey should be in proportion to the population.

Table 4.1

Table of Recommended Sample Sizes

Population size	Suggested sample size
10	10
50	44
100	80
200	132
500	217
1,000	285
2,000	322
10,000	370

Response Rates

Equally important to the sample size and design is the response rate. Researchers are often concerned about low response rates, which could jeopardize the ability to generalize or draw meaningful inferences from the data. Numerous studies have indicated that response rates have been declining over the years. However, it is not only the overall response rate that is important, but also the nonresponse bias, which is any possible difference in terms of attitudes or demographic variables between respondents and nonrespondents (Sax, Gilmartin, & Bryant, 2003). Studies have suggested that females, Whites, high-ability, and first- and second-year students are more likely to respond to surveys than are other student groups (Porter, 2004; Porter & Umbach, 2006).

Ways to Increase Response Rates

A good way to ensure a high response rate is to build participation into the requirements for the class. Course-embedded assessments that are part of regular assignments are likely to increase the chances that students will complete the assignment and that they will make their best efforts. Short of course-embedded assessment, conducting surveys in-class will yield higher response rates than web-based surveys (Dommeyer, Baum, Hanna, & Chapman, 2004). Dommeyer et al. (2004) also note that while response rates to online surveys were lower, offering a grade incentive could close the gap with response rates for in-class administrations. In addition, they found the results of student evaluations of the class did not vary based on the method of completing the instrument.

People may feel more inclined to participate in a survey if they receive something in advance or if they believe they owe it to someone to fill out the survey (Alreck & Settle, 1995). Some major assessment companies, such as Arbitron, will send a crisp one, five, or 10 dollar bill with the invitation to take a survey. This strategy, which is similar to solicitations from charitable agencies that include a token of appreciation, such as address labels or a calendar, feed off a sense of guilt or obligation for having received something for nothing. According to Porter (2004), prepaid incentives, such as enclosing a dollar bill, pen, or other small token with the survey itself, will consistently raise response rates, while postpaid incentives (paid upon completion of the survey) do not. Porter and Whitcomb (2003) noted that most research has found little to no impact of providing lottery-type incentives to increase response rates. However, Educational Benchmarking Incorporated (2006) found that providing incentives can increase response rates to its surveys by up to 6%.

Extrinsic incentives might include being entered into a raffle to win an iPod or a $100 gift certificate to the bookstore. If students do not complete the survey within the first 24 hours, they are much less likely to ever complete it. Thus, it might be beneficial to encourage students to fill out the instrument by entering their names in a raffle three times if the response is received within the first 24 to 48 hours. It is also important to note that the best incentives are things that students cannot purchase on their own. Having a $100 gift certificate is nice, but anyone can have that item. Survey administrators should consider prizes that will spark action, such as VIP tickets to a sporting event, a special parking pass, or priority registration for classes the next semester.

While extrinsic incentives tend to be a popular option among survey administrators, intrinsic rewards should not be discounted. Intrinsic appeals can be communicated through a well-crafted cover letter, which can go a long way toward boosting a response rate. A good cover letter will personalize the invitation (i.e., "Dear Sally" rather than "Dear student") and explain the purpose of the survey. Students want to know their feedback matters and that it will be used to make programs and courses better for future students. Toward this end, it is good practice when repeating a survey to highlight specific examples of how previous data have been used to make improvements or changes. Offering to make the aggregate results available may also increase response rates, as people often like to see how their opinions and perceptions compare with everyone else's. A good cover letter will also give the participant a sense of how long the survey will take to complete and provide contact information in case students have questions or concerns about the survey. Effective cover letters can convey an air of specialness. Porter (2004) noted, "scarce opportunities are often perceived as more valuable than common opportunities, so emphasizing to respondents that they are part of a select group should increase response rates" (p. 8).

The cover letter should also indicate whether responses will be *confidential* or *anonymous*. Confidential suggests that data will be linked to an individual student but will generally only be used in the aggregate. It can be very helpful to have student identifiers on a survey so responses can be tied to relevant student data, such as retention, graduation, or GPA. Linking an instrument such as the First-Year Initiative Assessment to an institution's student data file can yield a wealth of information that can be mined to further investigate the impact of a seminar on important student success variables. When student identifiers are requested, participants should be told how their responses will be reported and the safeguards in place to protect their identities.

Anonymous responses are collected without any identifying information. In some case, responses to demographic questions may reveal the identity of a participant, such as asking for gender, race, and course section number. If there is only one Black woman enrolled in a particular section, her responses might be easily identified if the data are disaggregated. Thus, claims of survey anonymity should be offered with care if one or two variables could be used to reveal the identity of a respondent.

Will making the survey confidential rather than anonymous affect the survey's response rate? According to Porter (2004), statements of confidentiality lower response rates only when the survey contains sensitive questions. Specifically, Porter found that strong statements of confidentiality can actually decrease response rates for nonsensitive surveys.

Finally, some thought should be given to the person who issues the invitation to participate. As Porter (2004) noted, "people are more likely to comply with a request when it comes from an authority viewed as legitimate" (p. 8). Thus, an invitation coming from a director, dean, vice president, or some other high-ranking official may elicit greater response than one emanating from a generic program e-mail account. Figure 4.1 offers a sample invitation to participate in a survey assessing a first-year seminar.

While a strong cover letter is essential, multiple contacts with participants are also necessary to increase response rates (Porter, 2004). These contacts may include some sort of prenotification, such as a postcard or e-mail informing the participant the survey is coming, as well as at least one reminder notification after the survey has been received. If the invitation will be sent via e-mail, significant thought should be given to the subject line as this can dictate whether or not the e-mail is deleted before it is opened.

Dear Sally,

A few years ago you participated in the University 101 experience here at the University of South Carolina. We are now asking you to take part in a survey to offer us some feedback in order to improve the program. Only a small group of former students has been selected to receive this survey; therefore, **your participation is very important.**

We want to make sure that this course is as relevant and successful as possible. As part of this process, we are seeking feedback from students like you to help us tailor our program for future University of South Carolina students. This survey is short and will only take a few minutes to complete. All responses are strictly confidential, so we appreciate your thoughtful feedback.

As a token of our appreciation, all students who complete the survey will be entered in a drawing to win a $100 gift card to the University Bookstore. Your name for the drawing will in no way be connected to your answers. Those who complete the survey within the first 24 hours will be entered three times for the prize. So you can increase your chances of winning by completing the survey right now!

Please take the next few minutes to complete this important survey about your University 101 experience! Your participation is greatly appreciated. If you have any questions or concerns about this survey, please feel free to contact me at friedman@sc.edu.

Sincerely,
Dan Friedman, PhD
Director, University 101

Figure 4.1. Sample survey invitation.

Populations to Assess

While the main focus of this book is on assessing student learning and outcomes related to the first-year seminar, it is important to remember there are other audiences who can provide information useful for understanding the efficacy of the seminar. Below is a suggested list of groups or audiences to assess, along with relevant topics and questions to explore with each group.

Instructors

Instructors of first-year seminars often represent a wide range of disciplines, professional responsibilities, and teaching experience. For most instructors, teaching the seminar falls outside their regular job description and disciplinary background. It also requires the use of engaging pedagogies with which many do not have great familiarity or comfort. Assessment can provide answers to help explain and improve the instructor experience. Relevant topics might include (a) satisfaction with teaching; (b) satisfaction with the level of support and faculty development provided (and suggestions for improvement); (c) satisfaction and feedback regarding curricular materials (i.e., textbooks) or classroom space; and (d) impact of teaching the seminar on other areas of their work, such as greater knowledge of students and their needs or the application of more diverse and interactive teaching strategies to other courses taught. Below is a list of instructor outcomes that may be affected by their experience teaching the seminar.

As a result of teaching University 101, I ...

- » Use a wider variety of teaching strategies
- » Lecture less and facilitate discussion more
- » Am more confident and comfortable regarding my teaching skills
- » Have modified the content of my course syllabi in my discipline
- » Am more satisfied with this institution
- » Am more satisfied with my professional position
- » Feel more connected to this University
- » Have a better understanding of the University's mission
- » Have a better understanding of students
- » Am more understanding of students' academic needs
- » Feel more committed to students as a whole
- » Relate better to students

Teaching University 101 has ...

- » Provided me an opportunity to interact positively with students
- » Rejuvenated my professional work
- » Increased my network of colleagues within the institution
- » Provided me intellectual stimulation
- » Helped me develop skills or knowledge that I can apply to my other responsibilities

Faculty or Administrators Who Do Not Teach the Seminar

It can also be instructive to hear from faculty and administrators who are not involved with the seminar. Bringing in their perspectives can be an important way to gain buy-in for the seminar and to increase the diversity of perspectives about the efficacy and needs of the seminar. It could be useful to ask this group one or more of the following questions:

» How can the seminar better meet the needs of students?
» What are the most pressing needs to address in the seminar?
» What issues should the seminar address in order to ensure its relevance?
» Why do you choose not to teach the first-year seminar?
» What is your perception of the seminar?

Former Students

Upcraft et al. (2005) noted that "the goals of many first-year efforts are unlikely to be realized in the short term, meaning that assessment should be conducted at some distance after completion of these programs" (p. 488). Thus, it is important to follow up with students after they have had a few years of college experience to apply and process what they have learned in the seminar. Possible questions to guide assessment include

» To what extent did the seminar prepare you for college success?
» To what extent do you still use your classmates, instructor, or peer leader as resource(s)?
» What was most and least useful aspect of the seminar?
» What topics should this course cover?
» What did the seminar do well? What needs to be improved?

Peer Educators

Many first-year seminars incorporate undergraduate students as peer educators. It is important to bring these students into the assessment process to determine what impact this experience has on both their own personal development as well as the effectiveness of the course. The following are sample questions to ask of students serving in a peer educator role:

Please rate your level of agreement with the following statements:

» I had a significant role in my class.
» I frequently interacted with students in my section outside of class time.
» I had an open dialogue with my instructor about my role in the class and/or course plans.
» I often met with the instructor outside of class for planning during the semester.
» I was not utilized to my full potential.
» I regularly shared in the facilitation of class discussions.
» I assisted with the development of the syllabus.
» The experience of being a peer leader was valuable.
» My advice was valued in planning for the class.
» I was satisfied with my relationship with my co-instructor.
» I believe I have made a difference in my students' lives.
» I was satisfied with my role in the classroom.
» If I had it to do over, I would make the decision to be a peer leader again.
» I felt I had a place or person to go to if I experienced difficulties with any aspect of my role as a peer leader.
» The training session in the spring was useful in getting me ready for my role as a peer leader.

As a result of this experience, to what extent have you strengthened your ...

» Interpersonal communication skills
» Presentation or facilitation skills
» Helping skills
» Leadership skills
» Confidence or self-esteem

Conclusion

Data collection techniques are an important part of the assessment process. Given the increased use of surveys to collect information on campuses, designing a good sample and employing strategies that enhance response rates can help increase the chances that students are not over surveyed and that participants will complete the assessments. In many cases, it is not necessary or desirable to collect information from all people in a given population; thus, sampling helps makes the assessment process easier to manage. It also decreases the number of students who are asked to complete a survey, which helps to avoid survey fatigue. Whether using a sample or not, ensuring a good response rate is crucial to being able to trust the results. The strategies described in this chapter provide useful recommendations for determining from whom to collect data, narrowing the scope of the population, and ensuring healthy response rates.

Chapter 5
Analyzing, Interpreting, and Making Use of Assessment Results

Using results from assessment is perhaps the most important, and often most overlooked, aspect of the process. Faculty and/or staff are often in a rush to collect and analyze data, without much forethought as to how it will be used, with whom it will be shared, or how the information learned will be applied. As the old axiom goes, "you can't fatten a pig by weighing it." In other words, simply gathering data (weighing the pig) will not lead to programmatic improvements (fattening the pig). Data have to be put into action for assessment to be useful.

The results of assessment efforts can be used to (a) build support for the program that leads to its sustainability; (b) promote the good work of the seminar to both internal and external audiences; (c) inform budget decisions; (d) market the course to students, parents, and the university community; (e) guide decisions regarding faculty development; and (f) most importantly, foster program improvement and curricular reform. Using results is so important that Banta and Blaich (2011) argued,

> an effective assessment program should spend more time and money on using the data than on gathering it. This means sponsoring faculty, staff, and student discussions of the data and providing support for making changes in response to the evidence. (p. 26)

This chapter addresses three primary issues involved in making sense of, reporting, and using assessment results. First, it examines the questions asked of the data (i.e., analysis) once they have been collected. It also provides guidance on how to make sense of the answers to those questions (i.e., interpretation). Finally, it offers suggestions for sharing the results of assessment with others and using data to guide decision making.

Assessing for Excellence: What Matters to Success?

To assess for excellence, it is necessary to go beyond determining the extent to which programs are successful to understand why and for whom. Simply knowing that a program has or has not achieved its outcomes really does not provide very useful formative data. Perhaps, the outcomes could have been achieved in a more efficient manner. Or maybe those outcomes could be attributed to two or three important ingredients while the rest were inconsequential. Or, perhaps, the averages hid important differences between subgroups. To make meaningful policy decisions about programs requires uncovering more about why programs do or do not work and investigating the effectiveness for all types of students.

The primary purpose of any assessment effort should be enhancing the quality of the program. In the case of the first-year seminar, program quality is inextricably linked to instruction. Thus, faculty development is an essential ingredient in a successful seminar. Assessment can highlight important areas of focus for faculty development efforts. For example, many institutions use the First-Year Initiative (FYI) Assessment as one way of indirectly measuring the extent to which the course learning outcomes are achieved. Course sections with the highest scores on a given factor (e.g., knowledge of campus policies, managing time and priorities, academic and cognitive skills) may be sites of exemplary instruction. By interviewing the instructors of these sections or conducting a document analysis, program administrators may be able to identify successful strategies that can be replicated on a wider scale. Top performing instructors on each factor could be asked to lead workshops for the rest of the instructors or contribute lesson plans and materials to a faculty resource manual. In this way, assessment allows for the identification and replication of successful strategies. Thus, assessing for excellence means knowing which approaches work best and then putting that knowledge to action.

In addition to understanding the most successful approaches, assessing for excellence requires uncovering the variables and aspects of the course that lead to a higher quality experience. Instead of measuring the program as a single variable, it is important to disaggregate it into component parts. Seminar effectiveness could be investigated based on course attributes, such as the day or time it is offered, class size, use of peer educators, or instructor classification (e.g., full-time faculty, staff, graduate student), among others. This type of information will allow programs to determine what components to focus on for improvement, as well as make more informed decisions about structural elements of the course. The FYI can provide a custom analysis of the factors that matter most to overall course effectiveness. Table 5.1 provides the factors that best predicted overall course effectiveness for all first-year seminars assessed in fall 2011. Knowing the factors that matter most allows a program to focus on areas that will lead to the biggest gains in improvement.

In an unpublished study, Padgett and Friedman (2010) used data from the University of South Carolina to explore which factors on the FYI best predicted student persistence to the second year of college. The data were collected through a web-based survey at the end of the fall 2008 semester from students enrolled in University 101. Responses were received from 2,014 students, yielding a response rate of 72%. Results from the FYI were matched with information from the student data file (i.e., persistence and first-year grade point average) to provide additional outcomes to measure student success. To predict the effectiveness of these factors on persistence into the second year, a series of logistic regressions were conducted. A number of control measures (i.e., gender, race, high school grades) were introduced into the model to isolate the effect of each factor on student persistence. The regression analyses yielded significant effects on the sense of belonging and acceptance factor. A standard deviation increase in sense of belonging and acceptance increased the odds of persisting into the second year by 38%. Knowing that sense of belonging tends to promote persistence at the University of South Carolina has resulted in greater emphasis on this topic at faculty development workshops and the creation of new activities and lesson plans that foster this outcome.

Another way to determine what matters to success is to implement an action-research assessment design that investigates the effectiveness of two different pedagogical approaches to the same topic. For instance, does attending a library tutorial session result in greater gains than covering the topic in class via other methods? Table 5.2 depicts the results from a study at the University of South Carolina that analyzed student responses to questions on the FYI about information literacy based on whether or not the class attended a library research presentation. The results indicated that students who attended the library presentation were significantly more likely to report they have the ability to find what they need through the library than students who did not participate.

Table 5.1

Factors That Predict Overall Course Effectiveness in the First-Year Seminar ($N = 18{,}881$)

Overall course effectiveness factors	Impact on overall course effectiveness	Contribution to the total impact	Factor performance	Recommendation category
High-impact factors				
Course included engaging pedagogy	1st predictor	19.2%	5.03[a]	Top priority
Usefulness of course readings	2nd predictor	17.2%	4.77[a]	Top priority
Course improved managing time and priorities	3rd predictor	11.4%	5.00[a]	Top priority
Course improved connections with peers	4th predictor	5.2%	5.17[a]	Top priority
No/low-impact factors				
Course improved study strategies	5th predictor	4.7%	4.68[a]	Monitor
Course improved knowledge of campus policies	6th predictor	4.1%	5.27[b]	Monitor
Course increased out-of-class engagement	7th predictor	4.0%	4.46[a]	Monitor
Course improved critical thinking	8th predictor	2.2%	4.79[a]	Monitor

Overall course effectiveness factors	Impact on overall course effectiveness	Contribution to the total impact	Factor performance	Recommendation category
Course improved knowledge of wellness	9th predictor	1.9%	4.63[a]	Maintain
Course improved knowledge of academic services	10th predictor	1.5%	5.48[b]	Monitor
Sense of belonging and acceptance	11th predictor	1.2%	5.62[c]	Monitor
Course improved academic and cognitive skills	Nonpredictor	0.0%	4.38[a]	Monitor
Course improved connections with faculty	Nonpredictor	0.0%	4.98[a]	Monitor

Note. a = below goal (5.24 or lower), b = moderately below goal (5.25–5.49), c = above goal (5.50 or higher). Adapted from "First-Year Initiative Assessment Recommendations for Improvement" by Educational Benchmarking, Incorporated, 2011, *First-Year Initiative Assessment Total Findings Executive Summary.* Copyright 2011 by Educational Benchmarking, Inc.

Table 5.2

Information Literacy Means for Library Presentation Participants and Nonparticipants (N = 1,404)

Course contributed to (7-point scale)	Question mean (*n*)		*t*-value
	Participant	Nonparticipant	
Ability to find what I need through the library	5.42 (584)	4.63 (791)	8.07***
Evaluating the quality of opinions and facts	4.63 (583)	4.69 (794)	-.587
Extent to which the course helped determine the quality of information sources when conducting research	4.39 (579)	4.24 (793)	1.47

*** $p < .001$

Looking at Subpopulations: Disaggregating the Findings

When looking at assessment results, it is also important to ask whether all types of students experience or benefit from the course in the same way. Data can be disaggregated by subgroups based on race or ethnicity, first-generation status, gender, or ability level (e.g., predicted grade point average). Disaggregating data can help determine which groups benefit most from specific aspects of the course, which in turn may help better tailor the course to the needs of students. It can also drive important policy decisions, such as who should be required or encouraged to participate in the seminar.

For example, an institution might discover that students who enroll in a first-year seminar have greater persistence rates than students who do not take the course (see Figure 5.1). However, it is probably not enough to know that the course leads to general gains in one-year persistence rates. This type of finding does not provide much useful formative information. In fact, it could actually lead to misleading summative conclusions. For example, the institution might be tempted to require this course of all students based on

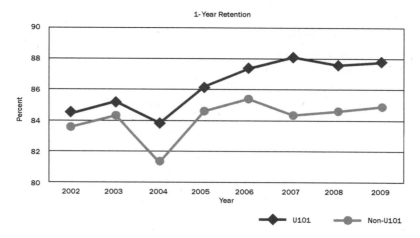

Figure 5.1. First- to second-year persistence rates at the University of South Carolina based on seminar participation.

these findings. However, by digging a bit deeper and disaggregating the inputs, program administrators might discover that the highest ability students did not benefit at the same rate as other students. Table 5.3 depicts how the one-year persistence rates vary by students of various predicted abilities. The left column breaks students into quintiles based on their predicted grade point average. In this example, the highest ability students who enroll in the seminar actually fare worse (although not significantly) than students who do not enroll. In this particular case, the top-quintile students who do not enroll in the seminar are often students in the Honors College. Thus, one would not reasonably expect to see a difference in retention for this group. However, the remaining quintiles show a marked difference in seminar impact. This type of analysis reveals a deeper understanding of the impact of the course on persistence than looking at all participants in the aggregate.

Assessing for excellence is ultimately about going beyond knowing the extent to which programs work to being able to explain the reasons why and for whom. While this certainly involves more work, the results are ultimately more meaningful and useful.

Table 5.3

First- to Second-Year Persistence Rates at the University of South Carolina for the 2008 Cohort by Predicted GPA

PGPA Quintile	U101	Non-101	p-value
5 (High)	95.0% (*n* = 383)	97.8% (*n* = 326)	NS
4	90.6% (*n* = 567)	84.1% (*n* = 138)	.05
3	87.8% (*n* = 550)	84.4% (*n* = 160)	NS
2	86.4% (*n* = 551)	77.5% (*n* = 160)	.01
1 (Low)	82.2% (*n* = 534)	74.7% (*n* = 182)	.04
All	87.6% (*n* = 2,773)	84.6% (*n* = 1,053)	.02

Note. Students without a PGPA were not included in the quintile analysis, but all students in the 2008 cohort were included in the overall retention calculation.

Interpreting the Data

Once data have been analyzed, the next step is to interpret them. In other words, what do the data suggest? What are the implications? Interpreting the findings should not be done in isolation, nor should it be done exclusively by the person(s) conducting the assessment. Involving others in the interpretation of data helps to ensure a more holistic understanding of what the data mean and creates greater buy-in. For example, Banta and Blaich (2011) noted,

> If faculty do not participate in making sense of and interpreting assessment evidence, they are much more likely to focus solely on finding fault with the conclusions than on considering ways that the evidence might be related to their teaching. (p. 24)

To interpret the data, it is best to consult with a larger group of people who can understand the context of the work from multiple areas. One strategy would be to form an assessment committee for this purpose. Not only will this help with interpreting the data and determining the implications and recommendations, but it will also increase buy-in for the program and the assessment process.

Reporting or Sharing Results

The purpose of the assessment will drive decisions about reporting, such as with whom and how the information should be shared. For instance, summative information used to make a case for more funding will be much different than a report detailing the formative findings that will be used to improve future course offerings. The information and reporting format will also be tailored to the audience. For the first-year seminar, relevant stakeholders might include seminar instructors and faculty, other university faculty, current and former students, parents, college and university administrators, governing board members, alumni, the first-year experience network and larger higher education community, and members of the general public.

Once a list of potential stakeholders has been compiled, the next step is to determine the information that each group needs to know. Different audiences are interested in different information; thus, it would be a mistake to send the same comprehensive report to all intended audiences (Upcraft & Schuh, 1996; Volkwein, 2010). Suskie (2004) noted several points to consider when deciding how to frame results to varying audiences, such as the amount of information a particular audience needs, preferences for how they like to receive information (e.g., text or graphs, hard copy or in person, detailed statistical analysis or brief highlight), and likelihood that the audience may feel threatened by the results.

Ways to Share Results

Results of assessment can be shared in various ways. Traditional methods include reports, newsletters, and presentations geared toward relevant audiences; dedicated assessment pages on program websites; e-mail blasts about recent findings to appropriate stakeholders; official college and university press releases; and inclusion in marketing materials. Care should be taken not to violate any confidentiality agreements stemming from use of national benchmarking instruments. For example, Educational Benchmarking Incorporated prohibits public dissemination of factor and questions means for comparison groups or peer institutions.

Another way to spread the word about results and findings is to embed assessment pieces into existing communications. For example, information can be shared at faculty development events about what was learned from recent assessments and what was done as a result of the findings. If e-mails are regularly sent to groups, such as academic advisors, one or two assessment findings could be included that validate the purpose of the course. An emerging method for widely distributing positive results is via social media (e.g., Facebook, Twitter). Social networks are an easy way to share program successes with interested members of the college and university community.

Tips for Writing Reports

One of the most difficult and complicated tasks of the assessment process is writing up the results so they make sense and are meaningful to the various program stakeholders. As Upcraft (2005) posited, "report formats are critical to the success of assessment studies in influencing policy and practice" (p. 484). Thus, great care should be given to writing effective reports. According to Upcraft, reports should include a meaningful title, an executive summary, a statement of purpose, a brief methodology, highlights of the results, and implications for using the findings. Descriptions of other essential characteristics of a written report are offered below.

Timely. Information should be shared within a reasonable timeframe of when the data are collected and at a time when the audience is most receptive to the information (e.g., share good news before budget decisions are made or share data that drive changes to the curriculum during faculty development events).

Relevant to audience. Messages should be tailored to the particular audience and include only the information appropriate for the group.

Understandable. Data need to be presented in a way that is clear to the average reader; therefore, it is wise to avoid using statistical jargon in reports for general audiences. Volkwein (2010) argued "the use of simple descriptive statistics, such as counts, percentages, ratios, and averages, usually conveys a more powerful and understandable message than multivariate beta weights, factor loadings, eigenvalues, covariances, parameter estimates, and the like" (p. 157).

Digestible. No one wants to read a lengthy report. As such, reports should provide small bits of information with a clear take-away message. Volkwein (2010) suggested reports follow the KISS principle (Keep It Simple and Short).

Accurate. Nothing can undermine a message more than incorrect information. Numbers should be proofread very carefully. Also, the numbers must be truthful and not misleading. This theme is expanded below in the section on using data judiciously and accurately.

Thought provoking. As mentioned previously in this book, assessment tends to raise more questions than it answers. A good report will prime the pump for readers to suggest new questions and to reflect on the implications of the findings.

Creating a report that achieves all these standards is very difficult. As Volkwein (2010) suggested, "research results can be accurate, timely, and audience friendly, but not all three" (p. 156).

Using Data Judiciously and Accurately

Deciding how to communicate numbers can be challenging. Including too much statistical information and jargon can discourage readers without such training. On the other hand, excluding relevant statistical information, such as levels of significance and effect size, could result in misinterpretations of what the data really mean. For example, a finding might be that participants of a seminar are 2% more likely to persist to the second year. However, without knowing whether the difference is statistically significant or the practical effect size, faulty summative conclusions could be drawn.

Even the use of basic statistics can be misleading. For instance, reports may combine two or more responses into a single category for analysis (e.g., percentage of students who agree and strongly agree with a certain statement). However, this practice may mask real differences, as illustrated in Table 5.4. In year 1, it is reported that 90% of students agree or strongly agree that taking the course was valuable, and in year 2, 100% of students agree or strongly agree. Thus, it appears that year 2 is an improvement over year 1. However, the means may tell a different story. It is possible that, in year 1, 90% of the students rated the course as a 5 (on a five-point scale) and 10% of the students rated the course as a 3. In other words, 90% of students strongly agree. In year 2, 100% of students could have rated the course as a 4 (on the same five-point scale), with 100% of students agreeing (not strongly agreeing). Thus, while the percentages appeared to go up from 90% to 100%, the means actually went down from a 4.8 to a 4.0.

Table 5.4

Sample Comparison of Means and Percentages (n = 100)

	Mean	% Agree or Strongly agree	% Strongly agree (5)	% Agree (4)	% Neutral (3)
Year 1	4.8	90	90	0	10
Year 2	4.0	100	0	100	0

Conclusion

Using and reporting data is perhaps the most important step in the assessment process. If data are not appropriately applied for continual improvement or shared with key stakeholders to advocate for the seminar, all the work involved in gathering evidence would be fruitless. Great attention should be given to how to put data into action and how to effectively report the results from the assessment efforts.

Chapter 6
The Course Review Process: Determining Relevance

Assessment is the engine that drives a successful first-year seminar. Without it, little can be known about whether or not programs work or what areas need to be improved. To be effective, assessment needs to be integrated into the design of the course and become a continual part of the improvement process.

Chapter 1 introduced the concept of using the right prescription (Rx) to assess a first-year seminar—determining the level of Relevance and Excellence of our programs. The majority of this book, and the assessment process itself, focus on the Excellence portion of the equation. However, it is necessary to ensure the outcomes in place are relevant to student needs and institutional culture, priorities, and expectations. This chapter describes a course review process to establish, modify, or reaffirm learning outcomes for a first-year seminar. In short, the course review is a way to determine the relevance of outcomes measured and may be a useful starting point for assessment. The chapter concludes with a discussion of 10 elements essential to effective assessment.

Determining Relevance[2]

First-year seminars suffer from what may be called the *family-attic syndrome.* As a need arises on a campus, it is often the first-year seminar that gets charged with addressing that particular concern. It goes something like this... "students are drinking too much, we need to talk about that in the first-year seminar" or "students are struggling with managing their money, so we need to add a financial literacy component." What results is an attic full of content that

---

[2] This section is based on the essay, "Assessing a First-Year Seminar for Relevance," an essay by D. B. Friedman that appeared on the FYA Listserv on May 22, 2009.

needs to be covered without the resulting yard sale to purge items no longer as useful or relevant as the new topics. The rub is that the majority of what *needs* to be covered in a first-year seminar is important, but there is only a limited amount of time available with our students, so hard choices must be made.

To determine what the seminar should include, a course review process can be implemented. The course review takes as its driving question, What do first-year students need in order to be successful? The steps for implementing a course review process are described in greater detail below.

1. Appoint a Committee.

To help with the development of goals, outcomes, and content of the first-year seminar (or with the work of refining these things), program administrators will want to seek the input of multiple and varied stakeholders. Some of the questions to keep in mind when identifying committee members are

- » What does inclusive look like on this campus?
- » Who can provide the right type of insight?
- » Are there skeptics who, nonetheless, have valuable contributions to make to the first-year seminar?
- » Who is entrenched in their position by defending their current stake in the course and would be resistant to change based on having something to lose?
- » Who are natural allies for the seminar?
- » Who represents a needed area of expertise?

Beyond individuals who might fit into one or more of these categories, program administrators will want to involve current and former first-year students, peer leaders, and instructors as part of the program review process.

2. Learn About the Students.

The actual review process begins with an examination of national, institutional, and course-level data to shed light on students' academic preparation, attitudes, and beliefs. The major purpose of this step is to educate seminar leaders about the students to be served and to replace anecdotal assumptions with data and evidence. In short, program administrators need to know who the current students are and how they have changed over the past 10 to 15 years. Projections about how they are likely to change in the short term (i.e., within the next three to five years) might also be extremely valuable. Institutional-level demographic data, grade point averages, residency statistics, course withdrawal and failure rates, and retention and graduation rates will constitute the core of information about students.

The national literature about first-year student needs, expectations, and experiences can also facilitate understanding about the local student population by situating them with the larger higher education context. Possible sources of data might include the CIRP Freshman Survey and Your First College Year (YFCY), the National Survey of Student Engagement (NSSE), and national data on demographics and persistence and graduation rates collected by the U.S. Department of Education's National Center for Educational Statistics.

3. Identify and Prioritize Seminar Goals and Content.

The next step in the review process consists of a series of brainstorming exercises that begins with the course review committee to identify the goals and necessary content of a successful first-year seminar. Each committee member is given 10 index cards and asked to write one item (e.g., goal, content, outcome) that should be included in the course. As a group, committee members sort the cards by category and theme.

To include the voices of multiple stakeholders, the needs identification activity can be replicated with other groups on campus, such as current and former students, course instructors, or peer leaders. The review committee can be charged with synthesizing the multiple lists to look for commonalities and differences. When this process was conducted at the University of South Carolina, 26 categories were created, including academic integrity, campus resources, time management, stress management, and information literacy. All were viewed as important, but they could not all be equally valuable. If instructors are asked to do too much, it is not reasonable to expect that they do it all well. Thus, the committee had to prioritize what *could* be achieved versus what *should* be achieved. One additional metric to help make this determination was considering those areas in which one could reasonably expect to have an impact.

A dot activity is one strategy for prioritizing the list of content and goals. Each committee member is given five green dots and two red dots. He or she places green dots by those items that should have high priority and red dots by things that should not be covered in the first-year seminar. The dots provide a visual representation of where areas of consensus about high- and low-priority topics are emerging that can guide the final decision about course goals and topics. The dot activity can also be used within stakeholder groups to get a sense of how students or instructors, for example, would prioritize the content of the seminar.

Next, the program review committee would reconcile the work of any stakeholder groups with its own deliberations to develop a prioritized master list based on the average ratings for each topic. This list could then be sent out as a survey to all seminar instructors and a sample of former students who would rate the value and importance of each item. The review committee might use the survey results to have one final conversation about the perceived relevance of each possible topic and begin the conversation about the language and meaning of outcomes for the seminar.

This process can be repeated every few years with similar groups of students, instructors, and staff and administrators to ensure that the content and outcomes of the seminar remain relevant. As students' needs and institutional priorities change, so, too, must the first-year seminar.

4. Develop Learning Outcomes.

Once the goals and essential content for the seminar have been determined, the program review committee can develop learning outcomes. One strategy would be to divide the committee into small work groups by goal and have each work group draft several learning outcomes associated with its goal. Because buy-in and diversity of thought are essential elements to the success of the new outcomes, the committee should share its progress throughout the process with relevant stakeholders to obtain feedback on the learning outcomes.

5. Map Outcomes to the Curriculum.

After articulating the desired end result, the next step is to determine how to accomplish the outcomes. This corresponds with step 2 in the assessment model in Figure 1.2. New subcommittees, composed of relevant campus partners and instructors, can be charged with mapping specific outcomes to the seminar curriculum. Here, they will want to consider both specific content and the process (or pedagogy) that will facilitate the desired outcomes. At this point, other course faculty and campus partners with expertise in specific areas may need to be brought in to offer recommendations or set parameters for achieving outcomes. For example, if the seminar includes a focus on information literacy, it makes sense to consult with campus librarians about specific information literacy skills, what constitutes proficiency in individual skills, and possible ways to teach and assess those skills.

6. Identify Needs for Faculty Development.

As noted elsewhere in this volume, the success of the seminar ultimately rests with instruction. Faculty must be adequately prepared to address course content in the most effective ways if students are to achieve the stated learning outcomes. Thus, it is important to review current faculty development efforts and resources to ensure they align with the learning outcomes for the course. For a thorough treatment of faculty development in first-year seminars, see Groccia and Hunter (2012).

7. Develop a Plan to Measure Outcomes.

Throughout, this book has offered strategies for developing an assessment plan. While there are many details to work through, the process is less daunting when thought about in the four broad steps of the assessment cycle: (a) determining the outcomes, as discussed in chapter 2; (b) gathering evidence, presented in chapters 3 and 4; (c) interpreting the evidence, explained in chapter 5; and (d) making changes based on the interpretation of the evidence, discussed in chapter 5.

Elements of Effective Assessment

There is no magic formula for conducting assessment and much of the process is an art as much as it is a science. However, there are clear elements and principles of effective assessment. Following is a summary of the top 10 best practices in assessing a first-year seminar:

1. *Measures what matters.* The assessment process asks important questions that reflect a wider mission and focus on clear and important goals (Palomba & Banta, 1999; Suskie, 2004).
2. *Is linked to faculty development strategies and decisions about the curriculum* (Palomba & Banta, 1999). Assessment should drive decisions about what students need to learn, how they should learn it, and factors that matter in creating and implementing a successful first-year seminar.
3. *Involves the active participation of stakeholders* (Suskie, 2004). Palomba & Banta (1999) noted that "widespread engagement helps guarantee that assessment will focus on the most important learning issues and maximizes the likelihood that assessment information will be used" (p. 10). It can also create buy-in for the seminar and increase the legitimacy. Using faculty and other respected campus experts in the assessment design and interpretation of data can provide credibility to both the process and the

findings, thus enhancing the reputation of the seminar. Faculty are often unaware of the educational aims of the first-year seminar, so involving them in measuring outcomes, such as writing, information literacy, or civic engagement, can help spread the word about the value and purpose of the seminar.

4. *Uses multiple measures.* One assessment approach or lens will provide only a small part of the story. Good assessment will examine programs from many angles and lenses to provide a richer portrait.

5. *Acknowledges there is no perfect assessment plan.* Even if multiple measures are used, there is no way to design a perfect assessment plan that will result in absolute truths. Measurement tools are limited, and studying human beings is inherently difficult. Upcraft (2005) relayed a bit of wisdom from his colleague Patrick Terenzini, who said, "In assessment, you start with the perfect design (recognizing that there really isn't any such animal) and then keep making modifications and compromising until you have a doable study" (p. 472).

6. *Balances efficiency with effectiveness.* Assessment is different from research in that it has a shorter time horizon and is narrower in focus. It is not aimed to be generalized to other campuses or contexts. Thus, conducting assessment may necessitate making concessions in the design of the study due to political, practical, or budgetary reasons.

7. *Raises more questions than it answers.* Assessment is never complete. It is a process of continually refining our programs based on what has been learned about what is and is not working, as well as honing an understanding about the efficacy of the seminar. In addition, the process of interpreting the findings should naturally lead to follow-up questions necessary to explain what the data mean. For many assessment leaders and faculty members, this iterative and ongoing process can create the desire to ask more questions before implementing improvement strategies. Banta and Blaich (2011) argued that

> one of the challenges of translating assessment evidence into improvement is for assessment leaders to know when gathering more information would help focus and clarify potential actions and when their knowledge is good enough to change a class or program. (p. 25)

The authors went on to say, "Waiting for perfect data or confirmation of findings ... must not lead to paralysis and fear of taking any action at all" (p. 26).

8. *Is valued* (Suskie, 2004). Assessment should inform decisions on important goals. Time spent (whether by faculty or administrators) must be recognized and honored, and it should be supported with appropriate resources to develop rubrics, purchase instruments, analyze data, and train faculty.

9. *Uses existing data when possible.* Campuses are often awash in a sea of data. Many times, data will be collected in one area that can be used in another. Whether it is information from the Offices of the Registrar, Admissions, or Institutional Research, useful data may already exist to answer many questions related to the first-year seminar.

10. *Communicates results widely.* Information has value and power only when it is used. Simply collecting information will not impact change. Data must be used and shared, and the decisions that are made based on data need to be communicated. In addition to informing others about the success of the program, it also demonstrates that the unit makes thoughtful, well-informed decisions.

Closing Thoughts

Assessment is a powerful process that fosters continual improvement. In the accountability paradigm, it also helps justify resources and establishes the legitimacy of our work. Assessment, when done right, should be a natural consequence of our work, not something external or imposed. Schulman (2007) eloquently noted, "I often feel that academics, in the face of the growing volume of calls for accountability, have developed a sense of higher education as victim, swept away by a powerful current over which we can exercise little influence." He went on to suggest,

> we must either paddle upstream, resisting all the way, or just go with the flow, adopting a stance of minimal compliance while hoping to find a little eddy in which we can float about undisturbed. But skilled white-water rafters and canoeists remind us that neither paddling against the current nor going with the flow is a particularly fruitful tactic. The best way to get where you want to go when negotiating the rapids in a fast-moving stream is to paddle faster than the current. (p. 25)

Schulman's metaphor is an important reminder that it requires hard work to get out in front of the forces driving the assessment conversation. The accountability assessment movement can be thought of as a train barreling down the tracks. Higher education professionals have two options: (a) jump on board to drive the train or (b) get run over by it. Either way, the train is coming.

Jumping on board or paddling faster than the current demands abandoning the accountability paradigm, where educators are forced to provide evidence of learning as an external, obligatory mandate. Rather, the focus should be on using assessment for formative purposes to help drive continual improvements to programs and to resist the temptation to take it on faith that what we do works.

Moreover, first-year seminars, which are rooted in a rich legacy of assessment and often serve as pioneers of best practices within an institution, should be exemplars of how to use data to inform and improve educational approaches. After all, assessment is the best prescription for ensuring the relevance and excellence of our programs.

Appendix A

Sample Assessment Plan From University 101 at the University of South Carolina

The University 101 course at the University of South Carolina has 13 learning outcomes organized under three over-arching course goals. While some outcomes are assessed annually, others are assessed biannually or every three years. The assessment plan draws on a range of data collection methods and lenses. The portion of the plan related to the goal of fostering academic success follows. The outcomes measured include

» Adapt and apply appropriate academic strategies to their courses and learning experiences
» Demonstrate how to effectively evaluate information sources and utilize University libraries and information systems for academic inquiry
» Recognize the purpose and value of academic integrity and describe the key themes related to the Honor Code at the University of South Carolina
» Use written and oral communication to discover, develop, and articulate ideas and viewpoints
» Identify and apply strategies to effectively manage time and priorities
» Identify relevant academic polices, processes, and procedures related to advising, course planning, and major exploration

Outcome	Instrument	Questions	Lens(es)	Timeline
Ia. Adapt and apply appropriate academic strategies to their courses and learning experiences	FYI factor – Study Skills	Degree to which the course improved the student's (a) Understanding of academic strengths (b) Test preparation skills (c) Ability to find items in the library (d) Diligence in reviewing class notes (e) Completion of homework on time (f) Involvement in peer study groups (g) Note taking in class (h) Ability to cope with test anxiety	Benchmark Longitudinal Standard	Annually
	Former student survey	Extent to which students applied skills learned in University 101 to other academic courses	Longitudinal Standard	Every 2-3 years
	NSSE	(a) Extent to which their experience at this institution has contributed to knowledge and skills related to learning effectively on your own (b) How often the students asked questions in class or contributed to class discussions	Benchmark Standard Comparison	Biannually
Ib. Demonstrate how to effectively evaluate information sources and utilize University libraries and information systems for academic inquiry	FYI questions	Degree to which the course improved the student's (a) Ability to evaluate the quality of opinions and facts (b) Understanding of available library resources	Benchmark Longitudinal Standard	Annually
	Additional FYI questions	Determine the quality of information sources when conducting research	Longitudinal Standard	Annually
	NSSE	Making judgments about the value of information, arguments, or methods, such as examining how others gathered and interpreted data and assessing the soundness of their conclusions	Benchmark Standard Comparison	Biannually
	Former student survey	Degree to which the course contributed to ability to (a) Find information sources (b) Evaluate information sources	Longitudinal Standard	Every 2-3 years

Outcome	Instrument	Questions	Lens(es)	Timeline
Ic. Recognize the purpose and value of academic integrity and describe key themes related to the Honor Code	FYI question	Degree to which the course improved the student's understanding of college or university rules regarding academic honesty	Benchmark Longitudinal Standard	Annually
	Additional FYI questions	This course helped me (a) Recognize the purpose and value of academic integrity (b) Understand the themes of the University's honor code	Longitudinal Standard	
	NSSE	Extent to which their experience at this institution has contributed to knowledge and skills related to developing a personal code of values and ethics	Benchmark Standard Comparison	Biannually
	Former student survey	This course helped me (a) Recognize the purpose and value of academic integrity (b) Understand the themes of the University's honor code	Longitudinal Standard	Every 2-3 years
Id. Use written and oral communication to discover, develop, and articulate ideas and viewpoints	FYI questions	Degree to which the course improved the student's skills in (a) Writing (b) Oral communication	Benchmark Longitudinal Standard	Annually
	NSSE	Extent to which their experience at this institution has contributed to knowledge and skills related to (a) Writing clearly and effectively (b) Speaking clearly and effectively	Benchmark Standard Comparison	Biannually

(Continued to p.88)

(Continued from p.87)

Outcome	Instrument	Questions	Lens(es)	Timeline
Ie. Identify and apply strategies to effectively manage time and priorities	FYI factor – Managing Time and Priorities	Degree to which the course increased the student's understanding of the impact of establishing personal goals (a) Understanding of the impact of establishing personal goals (b) Likelihood of preparing for tests well in advance (c) Ability to establish an effective study schedule (d) Ability to set priorities to accomplish what is most important (e) Ability to organize time to meet responsibilities	Benchmark Longitudinal Standard	Annually
	Former student survey	Degree to which the course contributed to ability to manage time and priorities	Longitudinal Standard	Every 2-3 years
If. Identify relevant academic polices, processes, and procedures related to advising, course planning, and major exploration	FYI questions	Degree to which the course improved the student's understanding of (a) The grading system (b) Academic probation policies (c) Registration procedures (d) Role of the academic advisor	Benchmark Longitudinal Standard	Annually
	Additional FYI questions	This course helped me (a) Identify relevant academic policies and procedures related to advising or course planning (b) Better understand the career exploration process	Longitudinal Standard	

Appendix B
Assessment Plan for Campbell University Freshman Seminar

Campbell University's Freshman Seminar (CUFS100) incorporates four student learning outcomes in its assessment plan:

» Students will identify their motivations for success in college.
» Students will describe effective engagement with others in the university community.
» Students will demonstrate improved ability to communicate through writing.
» Students will locate relevant information using technology and library resources.

The tools used to assess three of these outcomes are presented in greater detail below.

Learning Outcome 1: Students will identify their motivations for success in college.

Direct assessment measure: Students complete an evaluation to identify their motivation.

> *Type of assessment:* Course-embedded assignment
> *Assessment protocol:* In week 2 of the course, students are instructed to complete the 81-item Motivated Strategies for Learning Questionnaire prior to attending the weekly session.
> *Criteria for success:* All actively enrolled students (at the time of the motivation evaluation) complete the evaluation.

Direct assessment measure: In response to a prompt, students write a one- to two-page reflection on their identified motivation(s) to succeed in college.

> *Type of assessment:* Course-embedded assignment
>
> *Prompt for motivation reflection:* Based on the reading, your results from the motivation questionnaire, and your group discussion, describe what motivates you to succeed in college. What did you learn about what motivates or de-motivates you to succeed? How do you plan to use what you have learned about motivation and success in college?
>
> *Assessment protocol:* An evaluator (the FYE graduate assistant) reads and scores the motivation reflections using the Identifying Motivations rubric. Analysis of results is conducted by the assessment team.
>
> *Criteria for success:* Of the students enrolled in the seminar, 70% satisfactorily identify their motivations to succeed in college by achieving a score of 2 (fair) or higher for both scoring traits on the Identifying Motivations Rubric.

Identifying Motivations Rubric

Scoring Trait	Excellent (4)	Good (3)	Fair (2)	Poor (1)
Description of motivating factors	Motivating factors clearly identified and described in detail	Motivating factors clearly identified and described	Identification of motivating factors unclear or vague; description lacking in detail	Motivating factors are not identified nor described
Understanding of motivating factors	Demonstrates full and confident understanding of his or her motivating factors	Demonstrates understanding of his or her motivating factors	Demonstrates some understanding of motivating factors	Demonstrates little or no understanding of his or her motivating factors

Overview of Motivation Reflection Learning Outcomes and Scoring

The motivation reflection addresses the first and third CUFS100 learning outcomes: (1) Students will identify their motivations for success in college, and (3) Students will demonstrate improved ability to communicate through writing.

This scoring guide assists evaluation of the motivation reflection for learning outcome 1. The motivation reflection is the first writing assignment of the course, prior to any discussion on improving communication through writing. It is important that the evaluator focus on the learning demonstrated of outcome 1 in the evaluation, regardless of the quality of the writing.

Each motivation reflection should be evaluated for the achievement level of the following two items: (a) description of motivating factors and (b) understanding of motivating factors.

Learning Outcome 2: Students will describe effective engagement with others in the university community.

Direct assessment measure: Evaluation of engagement portfolios consisting of a transcript (log) of engagement activities, three engagement reflection papers, and an end-of-course engagement synthesis paper.

Type of assessment: Course-embedded assignments consisting of

- » A student-submitted activity transcript
- » Three reflection papers on campus involvement
- » An end-of-course synthesis paper on their campus involvement

Assessment protocol: Pairs of evaluators (blinded to student identity, trained, and tested for interrater reliability) review the engagement portfolios and determine if students have satisfactorily demonstrated effective engagement with others in the university community. Analysis of results is conducted by the QEP Assessment Team, using a 4-point scale.

Criteria for success: Of the students enrolled in the seminar, 70% satisfactorily demonstrate effective engagement with others in the university community by achieving a score of 3 (moderate engagement) or higher on their evaluated engagement portfolio.

Engagement Portfolio Scoring Guide

A CUFS100 student engagement portfolio consists of the following three items to be evaluated:

- » A student-submitted activity transcript
- » Three reflection papers on campus involvement
- » An end-of-course synthesis paper on their campus involvement

Each student engagement inventory should be evaluated using the following scale:

> (4) Student has demonstrated *significant* engagement with others in the university community
>
> (3) Student has demonstrated *moderate* engagement with others in the university community
>
> (2) Student has demonstrated *minimal* engagement with others in the university community
>
> (1) Student has demonstrated *no* engagement with others in the university community

Description of Scoring Scale

> (4) **Significant engagement:** Student has at least three engagement activities listed. The student demonstrated much interest and involvement for at least one activity. The student reported much learning and/or other benefits from the experience(s).
>
> (3) **Moderate engagement:** Student has at least two engagement activities listed. For at least one activity, the student has demonstrated some interest and involvement beyond simply fulfilling the course requirement. The student reported some learning and/or other benefits from the experience(s).
>
> (2) **Minimal engagement:** Student has at least one engagement activity listed. The student gave little evidence of interest in the activities. The student reported little or no learning and/or other benefits from the experience(s).
>
> (1) **No engagement:** Student has not turned in an engagement portfolio or has turned in a portfolio showing no engagement activities.

Learning Outcome 3. Students will demonstrate improved ability to communicate through writing.

Direct assessment measure: Evaluation of student writing samples completed at the beginning (preliminary assessment) and end (final assessment) of the course using a common rubric.

Type of assessment: Course-embedded assignments

Prompt for preliminary assessment: Based on the reading, your results from the motivation questionnaire, and your group discussion, describe what motivates you to succeed in college. What did you learn about what motivates or de-motivates you to succeed? How do you plan to use what you have learned about motivation and success in college?

Prompt for final assessment: Based on your experiences thus far and your goals for future campus engagement, complete the following Personal Reflection and Future Planning items. Your reflection should be in essay form. Through your essay, you should address many (at least 4) of the prompts below. While this is a reflection of your experiences, your essay should read logically and follow proper writing structure. Refer to examples of your involvement where appropriate. Avoid summarizing, and instead focus on the impact that your involvement has had on your journey to becoming an engaged learner. Your essay should be 500-700 words.

» How did you decide what activities and events to participate in?

» As a result of your campus involvement this semester, have you met anyone on campus that you can turn to when you need assistance or want to discuss a challenge? What relationships have you formed as a result of taking advantage of campus activities?

» In what ways have you been able to connect your learning from your cocurricular experiences to your in-class learning?

» What are the most important things you have learned through your involvement on campus and in the surrounding community? What has been particularly rewarding?

» How would you define an engaged Campbell student?

» What future opportunities are you looking for in your college experience?

» What activities will you continue to be involved in?

» What skills have you enhanced, or do you hope to develop, through your engagement experiences?

Assessment protocol: Pairs of evaluators (blinded to student identity, trained, and tested for interrater reliability using Cohen's Kappa/SPSS) read the writing samples and evaluate them, using a common writing rubric developed specifically for this outcome. Analysis of results is conducted by the assessment team.

Criteria for success: Final writing samples score on average, 0.5 units higher than preliminary writing samples.

Writing Rubric

Scoring Trait	Beginning 1	Developing 2	Intermediate 3	Competent 4	Advanced 5
Purpose Describes the intended objective(s) or goal(s)	Central idea or goal of the writing is not stated, is unclear and/or inappropriate for the task.	Central idea or goal of the writing is difficult to discern, or not stated explicitly but emerges from the narrative.	Central idea or goal is stated but somewhat vague, unclear or unfocused.	Central idea or goal is evident, and generally clear and focused.	Central idea or goal is clearly stated and focused.
Organization Coherence, format, order of ideas, transitions	Writing is disjointed (lacking unity and jumping from point to point) and poorly structured with no clear beginning (introduction), middle, and end (conclusion) and/or contains no paragraphs or poorly chosen paragraphs. Lack of connections and transitions makes it difficult to comprehend.	Writing exhibits some structure but remains fairly disjointed; uses paragraphs but sequencing (presentation and ordering of ideas) may be confusing and/or inconsistent. Attempts to connect transitions between ideas and paragraphs are poorly implemented.	Writing is structured in ordered paragraphs, including an introduction and conclusion, but there is inconsistent use and/or effectiveness of connections and transitions between paragraphs and ideas. There is inconsistent flow of text (smooth in part and awkward in part).	Effective structure and arrangement of ideas, using well-ordered paragraphs, including an obvious introduction and conclusion, with perhaps some awkwardness in connections and transitions; text flows well (smoothly) with few exceptions.	Organizational structure is clearly evident with main idea(s) or goal clearly and effectively developed in well-ordered paragraphs and with smooth and effective connections and transitions.
Content Relevant and concisely expressed information focused on the objective or purpose	Fails to develop main idea(s). Lacks relevant and accurate supporting information. May exhibit no elaboration or excessive wordiness; may contain redundancies.	Minimal development of main idea(s); little supporting information given, some of which is irrelevant (not on topic), inaccurate, and/ or redundant. May be excessively wordy.	Provides some accurate, relevant supporting information for the main idea, but details are general and elaboration may be uneven. May be wordy, containing some irrelevant and/or redundant content.	Provides accurate and relevant information supporting the main idea; generally concise and focused on central idea. May contain occasional minor errors; unnecessary, irrelevant, or redundant content.	Consistently presents a focused central idea with ample accurate and relevant supporting information presented concisely.

Scoring Trait	Beginning 1	Developing 2	Intermediate 3	Competent 4	Advanced 5
Style Considers the audience, circumstances, and purpose of the task, using appropriate terminology, tone, and word choice	Inappropriate and/ or inconsistent tone for situation and audience; unclear, incorrect, or inappropriate word choice (i.e., slang; clichés; and/ or impolite, insensitive, or colloquial language).	Several instances where tone and/or word choice are inappropriate, incorrect, and/or inconsistent.	Only a few instances where tone and/or word choice are inappropriate, incorrect, and/or inconsistent.	Generally consistent and appropriate tone for situation and audience; generally clear and appropriate word choice.	Tone and word choice is always consistent and appropriate in regard to the audience and purpose of the task.

References

Alreck, P. L., & Settle, R. B. (1995). *The survey research handbook* (2nd ed.). New York, NY: McGraw-Hill.

Anderson, L. (2005). Objectives, evaluation, and the improvement of education. *Studies in Educational Evaluation, 31,* 102-113.

Anderson, L. W., & Krathwohl, D. R. (2001). *A taxonomy for learning, teaching, and assessing: A revision of Bloom's taxonomy of educational objectives.* New York, NY: Longman.

Angelo, T. (1995, November 7). Definition of assessment. *AAHE Bulletin, 48*(3), 7.

Arum, R., & Roksa, J. (2011). *Academically adrift: Limited learning on college campuses.* Chicago, IL: University of Chicago Press.

Astin, A. W. (1993). *Assessment for excellence: The philosophy and practice of assessment and evaluation in higher education.* Phoenix, AZ: American Council on Education and The Oryx Press.

Astin, A. W., Banta, T. W., Cross, K. P., El-Khawas, E., Ewell, P. T., Hutchings, P., et al. (1996). *9 principles of good practice for assessing student learning.* Washington, DC: American Association of Higher Education.

Banta, T. W., & Blaich, C. (2011). Closing the assessment loop. *Change, 43*(1), 22-27.

Banta, T. W., Jones, E. A., & Black, K. E. (2009). *Designing effective assessment: Principles and profiles of good practice.* San Francisco, CA: Jossey-Bass.

Barefoot, B. O. (Ed.). (1993). *Exploring the evidence: Reporting outcomes of freshman seminars* (Monograph No. 11). Columbia, SC: University of South Carolina, National Resource Center for The Freshman Year Experience.

Barefoot, B. O., Warnock, C. L., Dickinson, M. P., Richardson, S. E., & Roberts, M. R. (Eds.). (1998). *Exploring the evidence: Reporting outcomes of first-year seminars, Volume II* (Monograph No. 25). Columbia, SC: University of South Carolina, National Resource Center for The First-Year Experience and Students in Transition.

Bernard, H. (2002). *Research methods in anthropology.* Walnut Creek, CA: Alta Mira Press.

Blaich, C., & Wise, K. (2011). *From gathering to using assessment results: Lessons from the Wabash National Study.* Occasional Paper # 8. Champaign, IL: National Institute for Learning Outcomes Assessment.

Covey, S. (1989). *7 habits of highly effective people*. New York, NY: Simon & Schuster.

Cuseo, J. B. (2001). Course-evaluation surveys and the first-year seminar: Recommendations for use. In R. L. Swing (Ed.), *Proving and improving: Strategies for assessing the first college year* (Monograph No. 33, pp. 65-74). Columbia, SC: University of South Carolina, National Resource Center for The First-Year Experience and Students in Transition.

Dommeyer, C. J., Baum, P., Hanna, R. W., & Chapman, K. S. (2004). Gathering faculty teaching evaluations by in-class and online surveys: Their effects on response rates and evaluations. *Assessment & Evaluation in Higher Education, 29*, 611-623.

Educational Benchmarking, Incorporated. (2006). *Incentives used in EBI Benchmarking studies for 2006.* Springfield, MO: Author.

Educational Benchmarking, Incorporated. (2011). First-Year Initiative Assessment recommendations for improvement [table]. *First-Year Initiative Assessment total findings executive summary.* Springfield, MO: Author.

Erwin, T. (1991). *Assessing student learning and development: A guide to the principles, goals, and methods of determining college outcomes*. San Francisco, CA: Jossey-Bass.

Evans, N. J., Forney, D. S., & Guido-DiBrito, F. (1998). *Student development in college: Theory, research, and practice*. San Francisco, CA: Jossey-Bass.

Ewell, P. T. (2009). Assessment and accountability in America today: Background and context. In V. M. H. Borden & G. R. Pike (Eds.), *Assessing and accounting for student learning: Beyond the Spellings Commission* (New Directions for Institutional Research, Assessment Supplement 2007, pp. 7-17). San Francisco, CA: Jossey-Bass.

Friedman, D. B. (2009, May 22). Assessing a first-year seminar for relevance [Electronic mailing list post]. Retrieved from http://listserv.sc.edu/wa.cgi?A2=ind0905D&L=FYA-LIST&F=&S=&P=73

Gahagan, J., Dingfelder, J., & Pei, K. (2010). *A faculty and staff guide to creating learning outcomes*. Columbia, SC: National Resource Center for the First-Year Experience and Students in Transition.

Garner, B. (2012). *The first-year seminar: Designing, implementing, and assessing courses to support learning and success: Vol. III. Teaching in the first-year seminar.* Columbia, SC: University of South Carolina, National Resource Center for the First-Year Experience and Students in Transition.

Griffin, A. M., & Romm, J. (Eds.). (2008). *Exploring the evidence: Reporting outcomes of first-year seminars, Volume IV.* Columbia, SC: University of South Carolina, National Resource Center for The First-Year Experience and Students in Transition. Retrieved from http://www.sc.edu/fye/resources/fyr/research_publications.html

Griffin, M. (2009). What is a rubric? *Assessment Update, 21*(6), 4,13.

Groccia, J. E. & Hunter, M. S. (2012). *The first-year seminar: Designing, implementing, and assessing courses to support learning and success: Vol. II. Instructor training and development*. Columbia, SC: University of South Carolina, National Resource Center for the First-Year Experience and Students in Transition.

Heckel, R. V., Hiers, J. M., Finegold, B., & Zuidema, J. (1973). *University 101: An educational experiment*. Columbia, SC: University of South Carolina, Social Problems Research Institute.

Henry, G. T. (1990). *Practical sampling*. Newbury Park, CA: SAGE Publications.

Hersch, R. (2005, November). What does college teach? *Atlantic Monthly*, pp. 140-143.

Krueger, R. A., & Casey, M. A. (2009). *Focus groups: A practical guide for applied research*. Thousand Oaks, CA: SAGE Publications.

Lincoln, Y. S., & Guba, E. G. (1985). *Naturalistic inquiry*. Newbury Park, CA: SAGE Publications.

Maki, P. (2004). *Assessing for learning: Building a sustainable commitment across the institution*. Sterling, VA: Stylus Publishing.

Mlodinow, L. (2008). *The drunkard's walk: How randomness rules our lives*. New York, NY: Vintage Books.

Morris, L. V., & Cutright, M. (2005). University of South Carolina: Creator and standard-bearer of the first-year experience. In B. O. Barefoot, J. N. Gardner, M. Cutright, L. V. Morris, C. C. Schroeder, S. W. Schwartz, et al., *Achieving and sustaining institutional excellence for the first year of college* (pp. 349-376). San Francisco, CA: Jossey-Bass.

Ory, J. (1994). Suggestions for deciding between commercially available and locally developed assessment instruments. In Transition Research Institute at Illinois, *Evaluation technical assistance: Dissemination series* (pp. 396-407). Champaign, IL: Author. Retrieved from http://www.ed.uiuc.edu/sped/tri/ory.html

Padgett, R. D., & Friedman, D. B. (2010). *Relationship of FYI factors and persistence for University 101 Students*. Unpublished study. Columbia, SC: University of South Carolina.

Padgett, R. D., & Keup, J. R. (2011). *2009 National survey of first-year seminars: Ongoing efforts to support students in transition* (Research Reports on College Transitions, No. 2). Columbia, SC: University of South Carolina, National Center for The First-Year Experience and Students in Transition.

Palomba, C., & Banta, T. W. (1999). *Assessment essentials*. San Francisco, CA: Jossey-Bass.

Patten, M. L. (1998). *Questionnaire research: A practical guide*. Los Angeles, CA: Pyrczak Publishing.

Patton, M. (2002). *Qualitative research and evaluation methods* (3rd ed.). Thousand Oaks, CA: SAGE.

Pike, G. (2009). Assessing program outcomes in the absence of random selection for participants. *Assessment Update, 21*(6), 11-13.

Porter, S. R. (2004). Raising response rates: What works? In S. R. Porter (Ed.), *Overcoming survey research problems* (New Directions in Institutional Research No. 121, pp. 5-21). San Francisco, CA: Jossey-Bass.

Porter, S. R., & Swing, R. L. (2006). Understanding how first-year seminars affect persistence. *Research in Higher Education , 47*(1), 89-109.

Porter, S. R., & Umbach, P. D. (2006). Student survey response rates across institutions: Why do they vary? *Research in Higher Education, 47*(2), 229-247.

Porter, S. R., & Whitcomb, M. E. (2003). The impact of lottery incentives on student survey response rates. *Research in Higher Education, 44*(4), 389-407.

Rhodes, T. L. (2010). *Assessing outcomes and improving achievements: Tips and tools for using rubrics.* Washington, DC: Association of American Colleges and Universities.

Sax, L. J., Gilmartin, S. K., & Bryant, A. N. (2003). Assessing response rates and nonresponse bias in web and paper surveys. *Research in Higher Education, 44*(4), 409-432.

Schuh, J. (2009). *Assessment methods for student affairs.* San Francisco, CA: Jossey-Bass.

Schulman, L. (2007, January/February). Counting and recounting: Assessment and the quest for accountability. *Change*, 20-25.

Skipper, T. L. (2005). *Student development in the first college year: A primer for college educators.* Columbia, SC: University of South Carolina, National Center for The First-Year Experience and Students in Transition.

Suskie, L. (2004). *Assessing student learning: A common sense guide.* San Francisco, CA: Jossey-Bass.

Swing, R. L. (2001). *Proving and improving: Strategies for assessing the first college year* (Monograph No. 33). Columbia, SC: University of South Carolina, National Resource Center for The First-Year Experience and Students in Transition.

Tobolowsky, B. F., Cox, B. E., & Wagner, M. T. (Eds.). (2005). *Exploring the evidence: Reporting outcomes of first-year seminars, Volume III* (Monograph No. 42). Columbia, SC: University of South Carolina, National Resource Center for The First-Year Experience and Students in Transition.

University of South Carolina. (2010). *University 101 faculty resource manual 2.0.* Columbia, SC: University 101 Programs, Author.

Upcraft, M. L. (2005). Assessing the first year of college. In M. L. Upcraft, J. N. Gardner, & B. O. Barefoot, *Challenging and supporting the first-year student: A handbook for improving the first year of college* (pp. 469-485). San Francisco, CA: Jossey-Bass.

Upcraft, M. L., Ishler, J. L., & Swing, R. L. (2005). A beginner's guide for assesing the first college year. In M. L. Upcraft, J. N. Gardner, & B. O. Barefoot, *Challenging and supporting the first-year student* (pp. 486-500). San Francisco, CA: Jossey-Bass.

Upcraft, M. L., & Schuh, J. H. (1996). *Assessment in student affairs: A guide for practitioners.* San Francisco, CA: Jossey-Bass.

Volkwein, J. F. (2010). Reporting research results effectively. In J. F. Volkwein (Ed.), *Assessing student outcomes: Why, who, what, how?* (New Directions for Institutional Research, Assessment Supplment 2009, pp.155-163). San Francisco, CA: Jossey-Bass.

Walvoord, B. E. (2004). *Assessment clear and simple: A practical guide for institutions, departments, and general education.* San Francisco, CA: Jossey-Bass.

Walvoord, B. E., & Anderson, V. J. (1998). *Effective grading: A tool for learning and assessment.* San Francisco, CA: Jossey-Bass.

Index

About the Author

Daniel B. Friedman is the director of University 101 Programs at the University of South Carolina, where he provides leadership for four academic courses, including approximately 200 sections of the first-year seminar. Friedman is also an affiliated faculty member in the Higher Education and Student Affairs master's program. Prior to coming to South Carolina, he served as director of Freshman Seminar at Appalachian State University and assistant professor of Higher Education. His area of research has centered on the first-year experience, and, on this topic, he has made numerous presentations, published several articles and monograph contributions, consulted with numerous institutions, and conducted a wide-range of assessment initiatives aimed at better understanding the efficacy of the first-year seminar. Friedman has served as an invited faculty of the National Resource Center for The First-Year Experience and Students in Transition's Institute on First-Year Assessment and Institute on First-Year Seminar Leadership.